DON'T GIVE THE BEAST THE ADVANTAGE

THOSE WHO HAVE AN EAR LET THEM HEAR

Rev. Anthony Martin
Author-Inspirational/Motivational
Speaker

The Kingdom Culture Fellowship Ministries
& Christian Self Publishing Co.

Copyright © 2014 ~ 2018 by Rev. Anthony Martin

DON'T GIVE THE BEAST THE ADVANTAGE
THOSE WHO HAVE AN EAR LET THEM HEAR
The 2nd Edition
By REV. ANTHONY MARTIN

Printed in the United States of America

ISBN 978-1-63273-012-1

All rights reserved solely by the author. The author guarantees all contents are original. No part of this book may be reproduced in any form without the permission of the author. The views expressed in this book are not all those of the publisher.

Unless otherwise indicated, Bible quotations are taken from
The Kingdom Culture Exploratory Study Bible
The Kingdom English Standard Bible.

www.thekingdomcultureblog.com

This Book is dedicated to:

THE IMAGE OF GOD

Be of sober spirit, be on the alert.

Your adversary, the devil, prowls around

like a roaring lion, seeking

someone to

DEVOUR.

1 Peter 5:8

Contents

Preface iv
Introduction vi

    1. Man's 24 hours. 15
    2. The Path You Take. 19
    3. When No Trouble, Don't Produce Trouble 25
    4. Good Cop, Bad Cop 60
A Message To The Community

Introduction

In spite of the many differences among Christians, Jews, and Muslims, they share a fundamental belief in God as compassionate and just. As a result, those communities have often nurtured people of extraordinary kindness and courageous commitment to justice. In contrast to the deep hatred that obviously inspired the September 11 attacks on the World Trade Center and the Pentagon, the vast majority of Muslims, like their Jewish and Christian counterparts, are appalled and sickened by terrorism, and utterly repudiate the mass murder of innocent people. Why then do some members of those same communities believe that it is their moral obligation to wage aggressive holy war, even to annihilate innocent people in God's name? What aspects of their scriptures and traditions tend to support violence against "infidels"? What ethical principles--religious and non-religious--can we affirm in response to those ideas and the atrocities that they sometimes engender? Religion is clearly not the only catalyst of total war and other forms of indiscriminate violence. People seem to be able to invent all sorts of rationales for mass killing without feeling the need to cite the will of God. For example, just a few days prior to the September 11 attacks, two young men from the Sacramento area each killed half a dozen people, apparently out of personal revenge. And some of the most appalling atrocities in history have been rooted not in religion per se but rather in racial or class hatred. There may even be a genetic tendency in our species, like that of our chimpanzee relatives, to attack and kill others for no reason except that they aren't "one of us. One of the Mosaic commandments prohibits murder (Exodus 20:13). Why is murder wrong, other than its obvious conflict with love of neighbor (Leviticus 19:17-18, 33-34)? Essentially because people are made in the image of God (Genesis 1:26-27, 9:6). One might infer from that idea that no killing of persons would be allowed at all, that the concept of human beings as made in God's image would entail strict pacifism, an absolute duty not to kill people.

Introduction

But that is not what the ancient Hebrews concluded, since many offenses were subject to capital punishment, a form of killing (see examples in Exodus 21-22). So perhaps we might interpret the image-of-God idea to mean, all persons have a basic right not to be killed, but they can forfeit that right if they commit a serious enough crime. This would also be consistent with punishing only those guilty of crimes (Deuteronomy 24:16) and limiting the use of deadly force to the defense of innocent others or oneself. This is probably what most Jewish people would affirm today.

One might infer from that idea that no killing of persons would be allowed at all, that the concept of human beings as made in God's image would entail strict pacifism, an absolute duty not to kill people. But that is not what the ancient Hebrews concluded, since many offenses were subject to capital punishment, a form of killing (see examples in Exodus 21-22). So perhaps we might interpret the image-of-God idea to mean, all persons have a basic right not to be killed, but they can forfeit that right if they commit a serious enough crime. This would also be consistent with punishing only those guilty of crimes (Deuteronomy 24:16) and limiting the use of deadly force to the defense of innocent others or oneself. This is probably what most Jewish people would affirm today. But religious violence can take on a particularly intense and ruthless character, if the objects of that violence are seen as blaspheming or insulting God, as the enemies of God or God's way narrowly conceived. The problem of indiscriminate holy war is particularly difficult for Judaism, Christianity, and Islam to eliminate from within because it's so deeply rooted in their scriptures and traditions. The same religious traditions that affirm God to be compassionate, merciful, and just, also include more disturbing claims that promote religious hatred and intolerance, and sadly have provided a rationale for aggressive holy war.

Introduction

We need to face these things head-on. Questioning the moral justification of holy war leads, moreover, to troubling questions about the legitimacy of some basic theological claims and the authority of foundational religious scripture. But collective punishment and indiscriminate war were also commanded or approved in the Hebrew Bible, especially in cases of idolatry. The first of the Mosaic commandments prohibited the Israelites from worshipping any other gods but Yahweh. God demanded purity and strict obedience, and idolatry and blasphemy were punishable by death (Exodus 20:3, 5). Non-Israelites who lived within the area believed by the Hebrews to have been promised to them by God were seen to pose a great temptation to them to abandon their faith. This led them to justify the slaughter of entire communities (Deuteronomy 20:10-18). And their holy wars eventually inspired similar wars many centuries later by Christians who admired Old Testament warriors like Joshua: "[Joshua's army killed everyone in Jericho], both men and women, young and old, oxen, sheep, and donkeys.... Joshua defeated the whole land... he left no one remaining, but utterly destroyed all that breathed, as the LORD God of Israel commanded" (Joshua 6:21 and 10:40). In the **Islamic** tradition, there is a similar mixture of values restraining war along with others promoting it. The Qur'an repeatedly refers to God as compassionate and just. It also says that "there is no compulsion in religion", submission to God must be freely chosen, not forced. The Qur'an urges Muslims to use "beautiful preaching" to persuade people to accept Islam and to "argue nicely" with Jews and Christians who are seen as worshipping the same God as their own. This is probably the attitude of most Muslim people today. Jewish and Christian communities have often been tolerated and protected under Muslim rule.

Introduction

Muhammad was said to have practiced non-violence early in his prophetic career but soon came to believe that God commanded the use of force, not only in defense of his growing religious community (Qur'an 22:39-40) but also in the form of offensive jihad to expand the territory of Islam. The word Jihad, by the way, means struggle or effort. Jihad can refer to the struggle of the individual Muslim to conform his or her will to Allah's, or to a peaceful effort to persuade others to accept Islam. But Jihad can also mean holy war. In fact, there's a sense in which the only completely just war in Islamic terms is a holy war since it has to be approved by proper religious authorities and waged to defend or promote Islam or the Muslim community. In spite of the Qur'anic statement against forcing religion on others, Muslim leaders have sometimes threatened to kill unbelievers if they did not accept Islam. Although Islam spread to some parts of the world like Indonesia mainly by means of "beautiful preaching," much of its expansion elsewhere was due to offensive war, first by Muhammad to unify Arabia, then by his followers in conquering Palestine, Syria, Iraq, Persia, and parts of India, North Africa, Spain, Turkey and the Balkans. Now, Muhammad and his successors did express some important moral rules for fighting holy wars: women, children and the elderly were not to be directly attacked (though they could be enslaved). Jihad was not supposed to be total war involving indiscriminate killing (in spite of what Osama bin Laden had claimed). But Muslim leaders were permitted by Muhammad to kill all captured soldiers and male civilians if they were not Muslims or had abandoned Islam. The fact that you might be a civilian or a soldier who had surrendered didn't necessarily protect you from being killed after a battle against Muslims was over. Thus, Islam traditionally did not have a generic principle of noncombatant immunity though many Muslim leaders today uphold such a principle.

Introduction

Of course, Muslims are probably as prone as Christians and Jews to seeing in their holy scriptures only what they want to see, ignoring other passages that contradict their preconceived beliefs. Someone inferring a mandate to wage indiscriminate, offensive war from Qur'an 9:5, "Kill the idolaters wherever you find them," could only do so by ignoring the particular historical context of that passage, verses elsewhere that urge defensive and limited uses of force only, such as Qur'an 2:190, "Fight in the path of God those who fight you, but do not transgress limits, for God does not love transgressors," and numerous other verses praising patience in adversity and nonviolent preaching. Turning to Christianity, its early history was characterized by a fairly strict form of pacifism. That approach slowly gave way to an acceptance of violence in defense of the innocent. And sadly, some Christian leaders eventually came to advocate force against heretics and infidels, and even total war in the interest of defending and expanding the faith. In spite of the loving and peaceful tenor of his teachings and example overall, Jesus did occasionally show anger, as when he confronted the merchants in the Temple (John 2:13-16). Some New Testament passages also appear to accept the institution of the military, if not explicitly praise it: Roman soldiers who met Jesus, John the Baptist, Peter and Paul were not asked by any of them to abandon their vocation (Luke 3 and 7, Acts 10 and 27). (Arguments from silence are notoriously weak, however.) There's even a passage where Jesus seems to permit his disciples to carry swords, and by implication to use them in some situations, though that passage appears only in Luke 22 and is very ambiguous. Jesus also claimed the authority to call on legions of angels to protect him, but held back because it would conflict with his sacrificial mission (Matthew 26). Paul in Chapter 13 of his letter to the Romans declared, "Let every person be subject to the governing authorities. For there is no authority except from God, and those that exist have been instituted by God." He who is in authority "is the servant of God to execute the Law of the Land on the lawless."

Introduction

But Jesus also set very high ethical standards for his followers, including an unbounded willingness to forgive wrongdoing, non-retaliation against evil, and love of enemies (Matthew 5). Three of the Gospels say that he rebuked one of his disciples for using a sword to defend him at his arrest. Most of his early followers seem to have interpreted Jesus' commands to prohibit all uses of force by Christians, even in defense of the innocent. Paul echoed Jesus' nonviolent message in his letter to the Romans, Chapter 12: "Repay no one evil for evil ... never avenge yourselves." Over a century later, Tertullian argued that holding public office and being a soldier would inevitably require actions forbidden to Christians; in his view, "It is more permissible to be killed than to kill." Hippolytus thought that Christians should not join the army; but if they were already in the army, they must disobey orders to kill. Although some Christians served as Roman soldiers during the Church's early history, a very significant shift in Christian thinking about war occurred in the fourth century when Emperor Constantine began to use the Roman state to support the Church. Christian pacifism was from then on to be strictly for clergy, monks, and nuns; lay Christians would now be obligated to discipline. Jesus' commands not to resist or retaliate against evil, although Christian love entailed a duty to use discipline to defend innocent third parties--indeed, a Christian who refused to prevent injury to another person would be as bad as the one who inflicted it. The focus of Christian moral concern from the act of violence to attitude of the agent: Christians should love their enemies, even as they repel them with deadly force! In effect, Roman military virtues for Christian purposes: risking one's life to defend the empire became courageous, just and noble for Christians. Augustine believed that there should be moral limits on war.

Introduction

Even in cases where Augustine considered war to be the lesser of evils, he regarded killing as ultimately tragic, always requiring an attitude of mourning and regret on the part of Christians. Partly due to his influence, throughout most of the medieval period, killing in war was considered a very serious sin. If a Christian soldier killed an enemy soldier, even in a war that was considered just, the Christian soldier would have to do penance for the killing, usually by fasting and prayer for a year or more. Beginning around the ninth century, though, another important evolution of Christian thinking occurred. Killing unbelievers was actually declared by popes Leo IV and John VIII to be spiritually beneficial for Christian soldiers: Their sins could be erased if they killed in defense of the Church. In the year 1095, Pope Urban II launched the First Crusade, urging European leaders to rescue the Christian holy lands from their non-Christian occupiers. He referred to the Muslims who then controlled Palestine as an "unclean nation" that had polluted Christian holy places. Killing Muslims became itself a form of penance for Christians for remission of their sins. Moral rules governing the conduct of war were abandoned, and unlimited tactics were permitted. No one was immune from attack by Christian crusaders; whole cities were slaughtered. Tragically, some advocates of aggressive religious war can still be found today in Judaism, Christianity, and Islam. What they cannot legitimately claim, though, is that their position is the authentic expression of their faith. Every major religious tradition contains ethical principles that are incompatible with total war. People of all faiths can agree, that innocent civilians should never be directly targeted, that indis-crim-i-nate weapons and tactics should never be used against military targets in ways that would produce large civilian casualties, and that captured soldiers should not be tortured or executed but treated humanely.

Introduction

This would be the hope that in our present crisis of civilian death in our communities across this great Nation of the United States. We can resist the temptation to execute the "indirect" and or "direct" killing of large numbers of noncombatants as "collateral damage" dictated by "military necessity." But take a necessary step toward achieving greater compassion on such things is the recognition and accountability of the troubling lives and the value of life embedded deeply within the scriptures and religious traditions. In many Christian worship services, it is a common practice for someone to read aloud a passage from the Bible, and indicate the end of the passage by saying, "The Word of the Lord is Blessed," after which the congregation responds, "Amen." Imagine that you are seated in your congregation of choice, listening to the following readings: "I will sing praise to your name, O Most High.... The enemies have vanished in everlasting ruins; their cities you have rooted out; the very memory of them has perished.... The LORD will swallow [up his enemies] in his wrath, and fire will consume them. [He] will destroy their offspring from the earth ... their children from ... humankind." (Psalms 9:2, 6, and 21:9-10) "[Thousands of angels] proclaimed with loud voices: 'Worthy is the Lamb who was slain, to receive power and wealth, wisdom and might, honor and glory and praise! I saw heaven wide open, and a white horse appeared; its rider's name was Faithful and True, for he is just in judgment and just in war.... He was robed in a garment dyed in blood, and he was called the Word of God. The armies of heaven followed him.... Out of his mouth came a sharp sword to smite the nations; for it is he who will rule them with a rod of iron, and tread the winepress of the fierce wrath of God the sovereign Lord." (Revelation 5:11-12 and 19:11, 13-15) "How many were the populations We [God] utterly destroyed because of their iniquities, setting up in their places other peoples. When they felt our punishment (coming) ... they (tried to) flee from it.... They said, 'Ah, woe to us!

Introduction

We are indeed victims of our own circumstances and that describe an enemy as your family friends and neighbor. Because the real beast is your attitude you must have words of a compassionate and empathy towards your family, friends, neighbor or the community. GOD deals with the wickedness of those who denounce GOD and or deliberately mock GOD in the sins of life. Going against the commands of GOD that one would lead the Lord to burn in anger over many who disregard His COMMANDMENTS. All people in any community must respect the Law of GOD first, then the law of the land, but DO NOT GIVE THE BEAST OF YOUR ATTITUDE THE ADVANTAGE...THOSE WHO HAVE AN EAR LET THEM HEAR!!!

CHAPTER I

Man's 24 hours

Man has a twenty-four hour time table he must operate upon everyday of his life. This time is as follows, 1 Eight hours to Work (to the Head)......2. Eight hours of Service between Man and GOD (to the Man) .....3. Eight hours of Rest (to the Husband). For the threefold position of the female, to line up with the threefold position of the male is as follows 1. Eight hours of Work...to the Head and Helpmeet.....2. Eight hours of Service between Man and God is to the Man and the Woman.......3. Eight hours of Rest is to the Husband and the Wife. The role of the Helpmeet is helping man maintain his position on earth as the manager of GODS business in the world, in other words manage the earth. As GOD laid out the purpose and plan with Adam was to manage the earth, GOD then said "It is not good for the man to be alone; I will make a suitable helper for him. Gen. 2:18. It is clear that in management of the great earth as great as we men are in our positions GOD has given us, it was fitting that we receive help better known as the "Helpmeet." The Helpmeet is uniquely knowledgeable to service, why because GOD instilled this skill within her, given her the quality skill set of knowing how to handle WORK. In every aspect of what she does, it is done in the capacity of helping; she can be CEO, Manager of any position held it will always result to helping to achieve the goal. Once given a platform the Helpmeet can quickly spring into action and began toward progress. It is vitally important that she has a platform from the Headship of man in order to perform her skills properly. Note even in the worst conditions she is able to adjust to assist the cause.

Once given the right platform that would best suit her skills, and would sustain humbleness in her that would enhance the Headship of the man to maintain his life before GOD, as he was created to do. The Helpmeets purpose is to measure the skills of the man, measuring his strengths and his weakness and build on them. The Helpmeet has been created with skills of enhancement that is naturally in her to help the man establish his Headship. During the "Eight hour of Work" in man's 24 hour service time frame of his everyday life, this means finance, home building, and business establishment. This is business management, which is a very important part of GOD's purpose and plan. Luke. 6:48. Finances is the number one root cause of today's family break-ups, which leads to home and business loss. "He who troubles his own house will inherit wind, and the foolish will be servant to the wise hearted." Prov. 11:29. Every man needs a suitable helper but not just need a helper, but a help meet that perfectly fits. The helpmeet is supposed to suit the Headship of the man and not prison him. Many women like to seize authority from the husband and take charge of his life and leadership of the home. Every domineering attitude and character will be a destroyer of the family and enables the helpmeet improper role in the man's life. She is supposed to complement the man and not compound his life. God saw the man needed help, sending the helpmeet forth to help the Headship of man. By implication, the helpmeet is to fill the vacuum in the Headship of man's life. She is to help the man in the areas of weakness. But many women instead of complimenting have become problems themselves, thereby, compounding the man's life. Every helpmeet is to be a problem solver to the Headship of the man, burden bearer not a burden the carrier. The suitable helper is supposed to make the Headship of man's life sweeter and not bitter. She is in his life to add spices to it. Therefore, every helpmeet should do what is necessary to make the Headship of the man life sweet and not bitter.

Man's 24 Hour's

The suitable helper is supposed to help the Headship of the man, to fulfill his dream and not destroy it. The suitable helper is supposed to help the Headship of the man maintain focus and not to lose focus by distractions. There is always the tendency to be distracted from one's vision in life. The suitable helper is a tension reliever and not a tension builder. The suitable helper is supposed to be a psychiatrist and counselor to the Headship of the man. The help meet is designed to be supportive and not subtractive. The suitable helper is a keeper of home and not a trouble maker. The suitable helper is to tidy up things and not make them untidy. A suitable helper should adapt to the Headship man's life and vision. A suitable helper should be good company to the Headship of man. The suitable helper is not to compete with the Headship of man. The suitable helper joins forces with the Headship of man to procreate. The suitable helper is a builder and not a destroyer. You should hold your wife's love by the same means that you won it. (Song. of Sol. 5:10-16). Men pursue their future bride with ceaseless attention once married the husband views marriage as a goal accomplished an on to other of life's challenges. He then gives his ceaseless attention to the job, the boys or anything but his wife. She on the other hand viewed marriage not as a goal met, but as the beginning of a relationship. She viewed his ceaseless attention as a down payment of attentions to come. He viewed it as a means to merely get her to say "I DO". The man really WON the love of his future wife. He looked good because he groomed his appearance for her. He smelled good, because he regularly bathed and gargled, and he spoke words of "sweetness" to his love. But give many husbands a few years of marriage and they let their appearance and hygiene slip. But worst of all the sweetness towards their wife is gone. The wife speaks out to her friends, "Things changed after we said 'I do'!" You must warm up your wife in the day with words of kindness. Buy your wife flowers on a regular basis.

Don't Give The Beast The Advantage

You should at all times establish family discipline with your wife's help. (2 Timothy 3:15; Ephesians 6:4; Deuteronomy 6:6-9) Few would argue that the wife is the primary parent involved in the daily task of interacting with the children. But God has placed the father as the head of the household and foundation of the home, and that means that you must work hard along side of your wife in establishing family discipline, that is you the instructor and the wife the teacher. Many fathers leave the majority of the work of raising the kids up to the wife. In child custody cases, the mother almost always get control of the kids, not because she is a better parent, but because she is the one who has been most involved with them. God commands fathers in Ephesians 6:4 "And, fathers, do not provoke your children to anger; but bring them up in the discipline and instruction of the Lord." You must be directly involved with your children. And then be careful not to "provoke" them to anger, because you have not really taken the time to understand exactly what happened and why. Some fathers alienate their children because they hastily dish out too harsh a punishment because they want to get back to their TV show or reading the paper. To these husbands, children are an interruption imposed upon him by the wife. You are the Foundation of the Home! Train up a child in the way he should go, even when he is old he will not depart from it. Prov. 22:6. Men you must exercise the express power of GOD working through you and me. The skills and abilities we were created with, to manage the worlds. To take on that attitude is to take on the Citizen of the Kingdom of GOD. You are the "FOUNDATION OF THE HOME"!!!!!!

CHAPTER II

The Path You Take

In the beginning, God made the heavens and the earth, day and night, and all the animals on our planet - for a purpose. However, did He create man as some kind of hobby? Have you ever wondered WHY you were born? Does our existence END at death? What is our ultimate destiny? Do we exist to rule the UNIVERSE? The culmination of all creation was to make us "Then God said, 'Let Us make man in Our image, according to Our likeness; let them have dominion over the fish of the sea, over the birds of the air, and over the cattle, over all the earth and over every creeping thing that creeps on the earth. Genesis 1:26. The Hebrew word for God is Elohim, which is a plural form, and for that reason, we find the One who is the Creator referring to "our" image. Amazingly, God consists of more than one being. As the Bible continues its revelation of these Beings, it shows them in a family relationship. Was Adam immortal? Human beings were created in the divine likeness (verse 27), yet physical. When Adam took his first breath, he became a living being. He did not become an immortal spirit on the same level as God, for Ezekiel 18:4 tells us: "Behold, all souls are Mine . . . The soul who sins shall die." (Ezekiel 18:4). The Hebrew word translated as "soul" is "nephesh" which is also used in reference to animals but translated as "creature" in Genesis 1:20, 21, and 24. How could God make man in his own image if he did not give him an immortal spirit? God made Adam to look like himself. He gave him a mind capable of reasoning, thinking, and even creating, although his intellectual powers, in comparison, are limited. Adam came from the dust, the basic element of the earth, which of itself is inorganic or without life.

Don't Give The Beast The Advantage

Our Maker had to breathe the breath of life into Adam to make him a fully functioning human. God put Adam and Eve in the Garden of Eden specially designed for them. There were two unique trees in that paradise, a tree of life, and a tree of the knowledge of good and evil (Genesis 2:9). Notice what the first humans were told: "And the Lord God commanded . . . 'Of every tree of the garden you may freely eat; but of the tree of the knowledge of good and evil you shall not eat, for in the day that you eat of it you shall surely die.' "(Genesis 2:16-17). The implication is that they could have eaten of the tree of life and lived eternally (1000 years). Instead, they chose the other tree and set in motion a world subject to the bondage of corruption, as Paul said in Romans 8:21.As soon as they ate the fruit, they felt different about themselves and their Maker. They were ashamed of their nakedness and wanted to hide from God. Their innocent, trusting relationship with God vanished. They had knowledge of good and evil, but it was not what they expected. Their ultimate punishment was death: ". . . 'For dust you are, and to dust you shall return.' "(Genesis 3:19). God cast Adam and Eve out of the Garden of Eden because of their disobedience and unbelief. They would now have to rest living from a world cursed with thorns and thistles. Humanity had started on the path to destruction. It did not take Adam's children very long to harness the elements to form iron and other metals. They made implements and constructed buildings. They developed a social structure. Left to their own devices, the children of Adam grew so depraved that God had to send a flood to cleanse the earth and start anew with the family of Noah. Because he has allowed us to choose (Our will) our own course, many people do not believe that a divine Creator exists. It is common to hear questions like, "If there is a God, why does He allow crime, war, and disease? If He is truly powerful, why does He not stop these evils? And why does he seem to HIDE Himself?"Many religions teach the separation of man from God due to "the fall." Our creation was perfect and complete;

The Path You Take

Satan manipulated the mind of Eve which led both Adam and Eve to disregard GODS command, causing a fall from grace. Religion will tell you that God had to come up with some kind of plan to SALVAGE His creation -- a plan to repair the damage. They would have you believe that he has been in a contest with Satan since that time and that the contest continues to this very day. But the Bible says "I form the light and created darkness, I bring prosperity and create disaster; I the Lord, do all these things. Isaiah 45:7. It is important to note that God is in control of Good and Evil! So Satan was a part of GODs plan and purpose which was set before the foundation of the world the scriptures points out. We are GODS greatest achievement, through the human reproductive process He set in motion, God has created countless human beings (regardless of the census stating of 7 Billion people on earth). Moreover, it is His desire that every one of us become complete in His eyes. The Rapture will begin the process when mankind's nature transforms into our complete nature. It is vitally important that we understand how God redeems us. Our salvation is by grace through faith. Christians are His workmanship -- created in Christ Jesus to perform good works (Ephesians. 2:8-10). Many religions would have you believe that there are NO WORKS involved in following Christ. Many Religions teach a person need only accept Jesus to receive salvation. This is not what the Bible teaches! Jesus gave Himself for us:" . . . that He might redeem us from every lawless deed and purify for Himself His own special people, zealous for good works." (Titus. 2:14). The Christian's good works stand as a witness to unbelievers, who will remember them and glorify God in the day of visitation (1Peter 2:12). The plan of salvation will come when Jesus Christ returns to this earth. At that time, He will resurrect those who have died in faith (1 Thessalonians. 4:16-17, Daniel. 12:2-3) and will bring their reward with Him (Revelation. 22:12, Matthew. 16:27). Their reward will be according to their works. (1Cor.10:17).

Don't Give The Beast The Advantage

How does a person obtain salvation? What motivates him to want to produce good works and to remain faithful to the end? Before we can walk with God, we must repent. To most people, repentance means being sorry. The Bible, however, reveals much more. In preparing the way for the Messiah, John the Baptist taught the necessity of receiving baptism and bringing forth evidence of repentance (Matthew. 3:8-11). Jesus preached repentance."From that time Jesus began to preach and to say, 'Repent, for the kingdom of heaven is at hand.' "(Matthew. 4:17). Peter cried to the multitudes in Jerusalem gathered to observe the day of Pentecost:"Then Peter said to them, 'Repent, and let every one of you be baptized in the name of Jesus Christ for the remission of sins; and you shall receive the gift of the Holy Spirit. (Acts. 2:38). The first step in salvation is a change of mind, recognition that your ways are not those of the Father, and that your sins have separated you from Him. Repentance means being sorry for having sinned and having brought about the death of Jesus Christ, who bore the penalty of our sins on the cross."For godly sorrow produces repentance leading to salvation, not to be regretted; but the sorrow of the world produces death. "(2 Corinthians 7:10). The apostle Paul recognized that he had been a blasphemer, a persecutor, and a destroyer. He wrote to his friend Timothy and said: "And I thank Christ Jesus our Lord who has enabled me, because He counted me faithful, putting me into the ministry, although I was formerly a blasphemer, a persecutor . . . but I obtained mercy because I did it ignorantly in unbelief . . . This is a faithful saying and worthy of all acceptance, that Christ Jesus came into the world to save sinners, of whom I am chief." (1Timothy.1:12-13, 15). Despite the sins we did and would commit, God was willing for Paul and all other human beings to be saved and to come to the knowledge of the truth (1Timothy 2:4). He is willing to forgive if we confess our sins and change our lives according to His commandments (Rom.10:9).

The Path You Take

Once a person has fully repented and been baptized, the Holy Spirit renews his mind (Ephesians. 4:23-24). The Christian becomes a NEW CREATION (2 Corinthians 5:17), who must no longer conform to the values of a world led by the devil. The Citizen of the Kingdom of Heaven must learn to live by God's Word, on Earth:"All Scripture is given by inspiration of God, and is profitable for doctrine, for reproof, for correction, for instruction in righteousness . . ." (2 Timothy 3:16-17). The Bible corrects us and helps us to discern our innermost feelings as they compare to God's way of life. Man has perverted the word of God, polluted his mind, and let his body degenerate. He has failed to train or has wrongly taught his children. He feels resentment and envy - even hatred - toward his neighbor. He tries to get more out of life than he puts in. Yes, why are we special? What potential does GOD see in us? "You have made him a little lower than the angels; you have crowned him with glory and honor, and set him over the works of your hands." Not all things are under our feet just yet. It took Jesus Christ, who as God came in the form of a human, to bring all things into subjection and to taste death for everyone:"For it was fitting for Him, for who are all things and by who are all things, in bringing many sons to glory, to make the captain of their salvation perfect through sufferings."(Hebrews 2:10). The truly converted Citizen of the Kingdom of Heaven becomes a child of God -- a member of a Family first known to man as Elohim. In the beginning, the Family consisted of only two Supreme Beings. Now, it composed of many sons and daughters who will receive eternal life. Jesus is the firstborn of MANY BRETHREN (Romans. 8:29)."Beloved, now we are children of God we shall be like Him, for we shall see Him as He is." (1 John. 3:2).Why did God create us? The purpose of man rests in the plan of salvation and his goal to make man after His own Image. God has reproducing Himself through men and women that He calls a Citizen of the Kingdom of Heaven.

When such a person, through baptism, receives the gift of the Holy Spirit, he or she becomes a spiritual son or daughter, though not yet spiritually born again until the confession of (Rom. 10:9). Through Biblical studies day and night, daily prayer, and the experiences and trials of life, the Christian grows spiritually. His human, self-centered nature is reformed and shaped into godly character. Then, at the time of the resurrection, the Christian transforms from mortal to immortal. He is born again. Only this time, he is born into the divine Family, and not into a human family. As he was once born in the image of his human parents, his spiritual birth is the image of GOD. The resurrected Christian will exist and be part of his growing family! This is the wonderful truth why God made us in the first place! May God bless you and give you insight into the meaning and importance of the greatest commandment ever spoken: "Love the Lord your God with all your heart and with all your soul and with all your strength!" (Mark. 12:30). So the question is where are you going and who do you follow…The Lord and Savior Jesus Christ by way of The Father Almighty GOD or are you of your Father's Business the Devil?

CHAPTER III

When No Trouble Don't Produce Trouble

An identity crisis is a time in life when an individual begins to seriously quest for answers about the nature of his or her being and the search for an identity. Most persons go through periods of defiance against authority figures. Part of this "defining against" authority figures is identity crisis. Though kids may make extremely poor choices when they choose to defy parents, they are often participating in a deep exploration of self that will help them determine what they will do and who they will be as they enter adulthood. For parents, watching a child enter the identity crisis stage is often fearful and difficult, since deliberate disobedience to certain standards may be inherently risky. Kids can unfortunately wreck their futures if they push too far away from parental or societal law; they could end up addicted to drugs or parenting children of their own far before they're ready. Nevertheless, most children must make this fearful passage to find a unique identity. When they are in the midst of it, this may be called the moratorium stage. In this part choices are being evaluated and explored, and there might be high incidence of exploration or various ideas, interests, career, sexuality, and etc. Once through the crisis a person has what is called identity achievement. They have set their feet on a path and determined who they are and what they want to be. This isn't only about determining a potential career. Such a crisis can be about exploring sexual identity and deciding what ethics and values are most important. Some people end up on a path that determines their identity without exploration or introspection and this may be called a foreclosure state.

Some social scientists feel that a foreclosure will precipitate an identity crisis at a later point, since little exploration about choice was made. Occasionally people who live in very restrictive environments have their choice made for them, and an identity is established without much choice or examination of other options. There are certain cultures that deeply encourage and facilitate an identity crisis. In Amish cultures, some communities encourages older teens to live in the outside world before determining whether they will remain a permanent part of the Amish community and be baptized. Similarly, some Roman Catholic communities now have changed confirmation to a later time, or encourage people to take time to consider whether they truly wish to be confirmed in the Catholic Church. Allowing an identity to emerge before making such important decisions seems psychologically sound. As mentioned, the identity crisis is not redistricted to adolescence and the emergence into adulthood. It can occur at any time, and many people label the "Midlife Crisis" as a crisis of identity. Some people find their values, choice, or paths inappropriate after major life changes like a divorce. Furthermore, nations and communities can suffer these crises too communities can suffer these crises too as they grow or respond to major changes. How a culture identifies itself and what it wants and holds dear can be part of a national identity crisis that may take a while to resolve and may be somewhat constantly in flux. This brings us to God and who we are in Him. **Gen. 2: 15-18**... The Lord God took the man and put him in the Garden of Eden to work it and take care of it. And the Lord God commanded the man, "You are free to eat from any tree in the garden; but you must not eat from the tree of knowledge of good and evil, for when you eat of it you will surely die." The Lord God said, "It is not good for the man to be alone. I will make a helper suitable for him.

When No Trouble Don't Produce Trouble

1 Cor. 9:3 Now, I want you to realize that the Head of every man is Christ, and the Head of every woman is man, and the Head of Christ is God. Before the fall of Adam and Eve God set the stage for them in the Garden of Eden in perfect form and atmosphere. In the Garden there was perfect peace in the family setting; Adam was given authority over the earth and in Adams authority notice in scripture God created Adam as a man and not a child or a boy because a child or a boy would not fit in such an atmosphere of authority. Only a man given authority by God would fit such a hierarchy position, **now there are five things God gave Adam 1.) Eden….2.), Work….3.) Cultivation….4.), Protection….5.) Gods Command…but there is five things God did first with male and that is 1.) the first human God created was the male, 2.) The first thing God gave the male was his image, 3.) The first place God place the male was in the Garden of Eden, 4.) The first assignment God gave the male was work, 5.) The first instruction God gave the male was cultivate.** Many of us coming up in looking at scripture believed that the first thing gave the male was dominion over the earth this is misinformation and has been the bases of the down fall of man's position and relationship on earth, is this attitude of authority first. If you study the scripture more carefully you would discover that the first thing God decided was not how much power and authority man was going to have, the first thing God decided was man's identity and What is man's identity? **"THE IMAGE OF GOD,"** It is in the image of God where all things in man starts, when a child is born the first thing parent identifies with is who the child looks like, as an teenager or an adult being a citizen of this nation of the United States it is a law that you obtain legal identification. Image is the essential key component of a man's life because image shapes character. As a citizen of the Kingdom of God being placed here on this earth you were given an identification to carry and be attached to you all the days of your life on earth and beyond **"THE IMAGE OF GOD."**

Don't Give The Beast The Advantage

This is to identify you as to what you are, why you are here, where you are going and How long you will be here. Adam was given the image of God, then instructions of what he was here for, Why he was here, Where he belong and how long he was to be in the garden "Eternally" (1000years), until an identity crises struck the garden. Devil embodied in the image of the snake sought to bring about a false identity, starting with Adams wife Eve. The Bible says that the serpent was more crafty than any beast of the field which God had made and he said to the woman— "Indeed, has God said, you shall not eat from any tree of the garden?" The woman of the garden said to the serpent, "From the fruit of the trees of the garden we may eat; but from the fruit of the tree which is in the middle of the garden, God has said, You shall not eat from it or touch it, or you will die." The serpent said to the woman, "You surely will not die! For God knows that in the day you eat from it your eyes will be opened and you will be like God, knowing good and evil." This is called "Identity Theft" when one seeks to rob you of what you posses, that you no longer posses it. Devil sought to take away Adams identity by manipulating his wife Eve to switch from knowing only the image of God, which "Good" to now knowing his image "Evil." Gen.3:1-5. This is "The Battle of the Culture" where many of us do not know who we are as we carry out our lives here on earth. Too many false identities labeled upon us than the righteous identity "Image of God", we are to raped up into these mediocre labels such as "African American," "European American," Asian American," "Latino American" all these different labels we honor and display upon ourselves beyond the "Image of God." If you declare yourself to be of God, then you are a **"CITIZEN OF THE KINGDOM OF GOD,"** first before you are anything else. The reason Africa is called mother and not father is because you came through Africa not from Africa. When you are born of a woman you come through the woman's womb not from the woman's womb.

When No Trouble Don't Produce Trouble

Life comes from the seed of your father not the egg of the woman, so Africa is not a "SEED" it is an "EGG." This is why it's called mother and not father, because Africa incubates life not produces life, God produces life, not a piece of land. **I came through Africa, but from my Father in Heaven who is the "Author of Life."** So any label you give yourself outside the "Image of God" is a false label and should not have any authority upon your life unless it is from God who gave you the life you have. For His purpose not your own purpose and plan, you don't know enough about this life to have your own purpose and plan, this is why God says to the people of Israel— "For My thoughts are not your thoughts, Nor are your ways My ways," declares the Lord. "For as the heavens are higher than the earth, so are my ways higher than your ways and my thoughts than your thoughts. Isa. 55:8; 9. Once the fall of Adam and Eve too place, devil then presented a claim to Christ of owning the world as he said to Him— "I will give you all this domain and its glory; for it has been handed over to me, and I give it to whomever I wish. Therefore if you worship before me, it shall all be yours." Luke 4:6; 7. See, Devil committed identity theft upon Adam and Eve when the fall of them occurred because he was the cause of the "fall." This is the greatest level of theft that many people fast on a daily bases in this life is identity theft, having to deal with your name or your life being almost destroyed by such an act as this. The pain of the process to recover from such an act, pain in the initial thought process of the since of lost, which an overbearing mental pain that leads to a physical pain. This is how things play out in this "Battle of the Culture" when the Bible says— "We don't wrestle with flesh and blood but with spirits and principalities." Eph 6:12. The Devil seeks permission to attack our citizenship in the Kingdom of Heaven daily and his purpose is to keep us from knowing who we are in Christ.

Don't Give The Beast The Advantage

If we lose our identity in Christ, we lose ourselves; we lose ourselves on earth we lose our life from earth because at this point you are easily led to do anything as opposed to what the direction of God would be for the purpose he placed upon your life. It is very important to know your intimate purpose in Christ, your purpose and plan is all a part of the "Image of God," why so much the "Image of God" because you are the seed of your Father and being your Fathers seed is vitally important too whom you look like. If Devil can get you to believe in who you aren't as he did Eve in the Garden then it becomes temporarily powerful for him to get you not to believe in who you are the "Image of God" first before dominion. This is why many miss what God is seeking to do in your life because of misinformation, false information that one can't get beyond. So many people are misinformed on how God work; many are seeking to identify themselves with some sort of image in life that they themselves can identify with. It is in the image of things that one seeks his or her identity, in a mediocre world and because of image the world loses sight about who it was created by and for therefore the world falls into an Abyss by way of the hand of God. Christ Jesus was sent for the restoration of the "Image of God" before freeing mankind from bondage, it was the image of God that appeared to be in more danger than man being in bondage. This is why the Bible says— "Meditate on God's word day and night, so that you may be careful to do according to all that is written in it, what are we meditating on day and night, the overwhelming reason to such a high level of meditation is for purpose of God's Image. His Image as glorified as it is maintains all standards in your life know the level of intense character, integrity, discipline, obedience and righteousness such that this 'Image of God" carries it has no room for many crisis. Crisis come only by way of the opposite of what Gods image stands for and the opposite of God's Image is simple wickedness or foolishness.

When No Trouble Don't Produce Trouble

But often times God uses crisis to bring us to a point of obedience that "His Image" can shape our lives that looking upon us will see God in our thinking, our attitude, our speech, our behavior and our action. This is why crisis is important to identify, to know which way God is going with the use of the crisis in our lives, to know what the moment of the crisis is for, why the crisis exist and how to apply the wisdom of solution to the crisis that it "works for the good of those who love the Lord." A crisis is not something we have many answers too, we often fall short in dealing with crisis effectively enough that this crisis does not return the same way twice. Crisis must be met with head on with only God given wisdom, that the spirits and principalities that enforces a crisis can be met with very Holy Spirit that will give you the power of resistant's and the ability to overcome the obstacles that accompany it. You must not allow any room for crisis to over shadow the "Image of God" in you at no point for the sake of growth, progress, character etc. You must live your life in these last days as if Christ is returning tonight, seeking or pursuing God knowing He holds your life in the balance of His hands, under constant protection from the wolves, jackals and snakes. For any attack that comes to our lives must first get permission, can you imagine that, your enemy must get permission to put his hands upon you. What an awesome God we serve, **"I MEAN AWSOME."** You must know and understand meaning of a demonic spirit having to get permission to touch your life, do you understand how powerful that is, and the process a "Demonic Force" has to go through to get to you. What crisis could you possibly experience without the hand of God not being a part of things to protect your life? Identity Crisis is not a means of destruction; it's a means of opportunity, an opportune time in God obedience, discipline, character and integrity which should bring about a perfect union with God.

But because of many not feeding the mind the proper level of God's word that your thinking is dealt with and changed so much so that discipline is the ruling aspect of your thought process. The main reason that we miss out on much of Gods directions in our lives is that we lack the kind of discipline in our thinking process, which would bring our decisions to a complete "YEA" and "NEA," anything beyond that is of the Devil the Bible says. Crisis should bring you growth from the level it began to the level it forces you to, why by force simply because of many of our stiff neck ways we allow to take root or stronghold in our thinking causing us to disobey Gods directions. The Bibles says— "Many are the plans in a man's heart but God directs his steps," Prov. 16:9. Crisis come by way of misinformation or no directions, we to many times find ourselves listening to our outer man instead of the inner man as the great "Marvin Gaye" would sing and that's where we fall in much trouble during the course of our lives. God continues to hammer away at our stubbornness to follow his instructions and many refuse to hear His voice or just not intimate enough with God to even hear His voice. Many bring about great damage control in their lives that in some cases it is beyond repair. We are in a time frame where it must be Gods way or you will be removed, we will begin to see that revolving door of the days when God remove you from for sin and those days are returning especially now that grace is on the scene through Christ. God no longer has to keep folk on earth to assure ones inheritage through a series of faith walks and prophetic deeds, Christ has covered all our sins of yesterday, today and tomorrow we no longer are in need of the New Moon Festival and Sin Offerings, we have been sealed with the Holy Spirit that guarantee our salvation upon our confession of Rom. 10:9. So to remove those who are in great disobedience God will do and is doing to keep many from loosing portions of their inheritance.

When No Trouble Don't Produce Trouble

For it is your inheritance that is the only thing from Heaven that you will lose parts of and the Bibles says that God loves us so, that he protects us from taking great lost of our inheritance. The most powerful and richest place on earth is the cemetery simply because so many persons have left this earth without fulfilling the purpose God gave to many to serve here on earth. So many ideas, inventions, cure for diseases, answers to things in this life that would change the course of time forever. All in the cemetery not even an ounce of time to exercise such power and authority that was placed in these persons in the unique way they were created to exercise. So we lose those possibilities to bring about other persons with God given capabilities to exercise their uniqueness of gifting being shown to the world that the purpose of God can prevail. Prevail in a supernatural way that we can make great strive in this life just as God is calling us to have, not slothful or slumbered and full of poverty but making the difference in the lives of your family, friends and neighbors as we were chosen to do so. A nation of doers not a nation of Ney-Sayers but to conform in God that the world can spot who you are not by a cross on your neck or a bumper sticker, but in your speech, your walk, letting that spirit of God within us so connect to the Holy Spirit, that the directions and instruction given to us from God, by way of Christ in which direct the Holy Spirit to bring life into all things. We are to carry out the same as to what the Holy Spirit has been given because he is in us to do so, so that which is in you must flow out of you in righteousness that the world is affected by it so greatly that God is honored and Glorified in the Majestic manner that He demands. We are the Kings Royal Priesthood and we were chosen to operate in the "Image of God" and have dominion over this "Earth," **NOT TO CREATE AN IDENTITY CRISIS"**

Don't Give The Beast The Advantage

In this life we must not focus on our circumstances. That is a biblical principle that "you do not look to the bigness of your circumstances but look to the bigness of God, for if you look to the bigness of your circumstances then the Devil will use that moment against you and accuse you before God of lack of faith and belief in God to by o you to grace protect and bring you relief of that which stands in your way," We are to look past our circumstances in fact we are not too recognize our circumstances. We are to commit our lives so great too the purpose and plan that God has place upon you and live the meaning of that which God gave to carry out here on earth. Any and everyone has a purpose here and it isn't "Crisis," that is what is used to put us in obedience or discipline in God that character and integrity rules. You must live by meaning, What does your life mean to you? Is it a game or joke? Is it real? What is your name? Call your name and see what you are known by. These things are meaning, in my life I know I am to make a difference in the lives of others, that's something stuck with me all my life as I went through my daily routines of just getting up to go to a meaningless job. Faced with every day crisis I was lost in identity in my youth, but always had the spirit to help someone, something that I watch my "Mama" and my "Grandma" do. It was not something that I recognize as my purpose it was just something that was in me to do as the days of my life went forth as a youth. The day came when becoming a part of different communities and new persons arose in my life that I began to discover the meaning behind wanting to help folk. It began to unravel not in your typical world like fashion where you are in the streets and someone just think they know you well enough to tell you about your life "No." It came by way of the life I lived in God, see, I realize by way of the intimacy I have with God automatically gives the Holy Spirit the access it need to bring us wisdom even when we don't ask for it.

When No Trouble Don't Produce Trouble

You think you pick up on some high level of "ESP" as the world would say that gave you insight to the life we live, but the Bible says God through Christ Jesus is the author and giver of life period. Who else then can inform you of life but the author and giver of it? As I began to investigate my life more it came to my attention that I have a real purpose here on earth and how did I find it, by the greatest question ever ask of me "What is your Passion in Life"? I stop a moment and had to put in some heavy meditation about that and of course the devil took root to that thought and began to squander my mind everywhere. I went after that question upon my own notion that I knew what I was searching for and found myself bringing on a headache, until I denied me and ask the Lord for the wisdom in this thing and as I began to remove me in thought. My though patterns began to open up to me and who I am and the thing I enjoy to do. That is help people, to make a difference in lives of people, I recognize the energy and strength I put into such a meaningful cause. Once I realize what this meant in my life, this was it, this is my passion, and this is my "Purpose." I began to feed this thing and bring it more to life as it must be, I studied Gods word on this and learn a deeper meaning on how it works from Gods point of view since He put it in me then the one to ask is the one who gave it "God," my life began to take a turn from "Identity Crisis" to "True Identity," the "Image of God." But once knowing this you would think life got better no, greater struggle, greater difficulty and greater attack. Why? Because we were in Devil's camp having a ball enjoying the world's lifestyle, chasing the wind of sex, lies and videotapes, festering in Devils mess, believing this was our way of life to live. When we were actually as to what the word of God says—whoever wishes to be a friend of the world makes himself an enemy of God.

This is where we are when we are not with God, we are against God and that's the reason for attack, struggle and Identity Crisis, we lose sight of God and become someone we were not purpose to be and so the hand of God come against you is enemy. When you step out of Devils kingdom then you become an enemy of Devil, in other words there is no neutral zone between Gods Kingdom and Devils kingdom. You are in one or the other and either way you face difficulty, but the difference in Gods difficulty and Devils difficulty is with God difficulty come grace, peace and official rest as long as you remain in Him. It will mirror public opinion and thereby be justified. The Nazi cause was also the same as White Supremacy in the United States. The 65th Congress left the circumstances evolving around this event for future generations to discuss. That generation is ours. The East St. Louis Massacre of 1917 is exhibit. A" evidence for reparations for past atrocities against Black Americans. Not as former slaves, but as human beings and free citizens of the United States. "It is the ultimate end of unchecked American Racism. From 1999 to 2009, among those aged 15 to 34 years, there were 106,271 homicides, 85% (89,887) among men and 49% (52,265) among black men. One major and hotly debated issue is firearms. Specifically, 81% (85,643) of all homicides were due to firearms, including 91% (47,513) among black men. Homicide is, far and away, the leading cause of death of young black men. In stark contrast, accidents are, far and away, the leading cause of death among young nonblack men and women of all races and ethnicities. Black men are 6 times more likely to die as the result of and 7 times more likely to commit murder than their white counterparts. One eighth of the population is black, but one half of all homicide victims are black. Their reduced life expectancy of more than 6 years would be improved more from eliminating homicide than abolishing any other causes of death except cardiovascular disease or cancer.

When No Trouble Don't Produce Trouble

The rate at which Blacks killed Blacks in 1994 was 876 times greater, and the rate at which they killed Whites was 164 times greater, than the rate at which Whites killed Blacks. Whites were twice as likely to be killed by Blacks as by Hispanics. Blacks were twice as likely as Hispanics and 71 times as likely as Whites to kill members of their own race. One quarter of the nation's homicides were committed by the 0.7% of the population who were Black men between the ages of 18-24. If there were no Blacks or Hispanics in the US at all, our homicide rate might be as low as North Dakota, or 0.2 per 100,000 populations, which is 1/49th of its all time high of 9.8 in 1991. Such an extraordinary homicide rate cost this putative Christian nation an extra 24,209 American lives in 1991 alone, and 800,000 during the 20th Century--a loss of life three times greater than all American WWII battle deaths and 200 times greater than the loss attributable to "terrorism" by Muslims. Black crime in America is real, it's present, it's ongoing, it's pervasive--and it would be far easier to correct than any war on Muslim Terrorists. So why it is not corrected? Why do we instead go to war against 1.2 billion Muslims in the world, when we didn't lift a finger to protect the 50 million WHITE Christians in Russia from the Bolshevists? Why do we continue to imprison 6% of black men in the US for trivial crimes, and possibly crimes that they didn't even commit, while NOT imprisoning the black murderers? For the last two decades, the affirmative action hires in our justice system have FAILED to even prosecute a third of all the murderers in the country, leaving up to a quarter of a million murderers free to murder again--and again. Whites, who commit only 5% of these murders, represent 30% of our prison population, so it's not White murderers who aren't being imprisoned--it's mostly black murderers. What is the plan here? What better way to create resentment by Blacks against Whites than to falsely imprison Blacks who didn't commit crimes while not imprisoning Black murderers?

Blacks murder six Whites in the US every day. Young black men are 175 more likely than White women to be murderers and 145 times more likely to be murdered. Blacks & Hispanics in America caused an additional 22,374 murders in 1995.

Genocide of American Whites by blacks and Hispanics:
> Proven by the US government statistics.
> Ignored by the "news" media.
> Took 200 times as many American lives in the 20th Century than Osama bin Ladin.
> Homicides per 100,000 populations by race:
> Whites = 0.7.
> Hispanics = 27.
> Blacks = 52.

The large variation in the homicide rate from state to state is due almost exclusively to the higher proportion of blacks and Hispanics in some states coupled with their higher propensity to commit murder, particularly in Washington, DC. People in states like North Dakota, Vermont, Iowa, and South Dakota are up to 1/100th as likely to be murdered as people in states like Louisiana, California, New York and Maryland and 1/355th as likely as people in Washington, DC. But the percentage of the population who are blacks and Hispanics in North Dakota is 1/33rd that of California and 1/58th that of Washington, DC. Every one of the states with a high percentage of blacks and Hispanics has a high murder rate, including California whose low percentage of blacks is made up for by a high percentage of Hispanics. The result is that Hispanics alone are a mortal risk to Californians which exceeds the risk of dying from tobacco smoke by two to three times. If the entire country had had a homicide rate equivalent to North Dakota's rate of 0.2 per 100,000 population in 1995, rather than 22,895 homicides that year, there would have been only 526 homicides, saving 22,369 American lives.

When No Trouble Don't Produce Trouble

Such a rate over the last half century would have saved more than 893,000 American lives making multiculturalism an expensive proposition for American Whites. But perhaps it's a boon to blacks and Hispanics who may have killed each other in even greater numbers if Whites hadn't been around to organize their society for them. Had the homicide rate that year been equivalent to Maryland's, 8,672 more Americans would have died, and had it been equivalent to Washington's 164,776 more Americans would have died. It's likely that Washington's rate would have been even higher had it not been for the 28% of the population there who are Whites. North Dakota is living proof that White Americans living free of multiculturalism and race mixing could have an even more stable society than Norway or Japan. This low murder rate in 1995 was not a fluke, because North Dakota's rate has remained the same or even declined over the last two decades. This is not a new situation for states like Maine, Iowa, Montana, New Hampshire, and South Dakota, either, because they have consistently had the lowest murder rates. And they also haven't been bombarded with multiculturalism, miscegenation, and the influx of blacks and Hispanics like the high crime states have. These rates are also equivalent to countries like Singapore, the Slovak Republic, England, Wales, Cyprus and Japan, which also stand as living proof that low crime rates aren't a distant and impossible dream. Whites who have not been bombarded with miscegenation manage to keep their homicide rate at around 0.7 per 100,000 population, whereas blacks who live in White societies commit 52 homicides per 100,000 blacks and Hispanics commit 27 homicides per 100,000 Hispanics. This is one of the most heinous examples of the chronic media bias faced by White Americans each day.

Don't Give The Beast The Advantage

This inexplicable and chronic propensity to cover up almost every crime perpetrated on, legal system bias against, justice system discrimination against, and to belittle every action by, the White Christian man must stop, now. The mainstream media openly supports "hate crime legislation" which would effectively benefit every American citizen except the White Christian man. It focuses on one crime committed by White American men against one black felon James Byrd for an entire year, while ignoring almost 2,500 black Americans who murder Whites every year. The rate at which black Americans murder Whites is 8.2 per 100,000 Blacks, a rate higher than the murder rate of all but a few countries, and more than 8 times higher than countries like the Czech Republic, Japan, Cyprus, England, Wales, the Slovak Republic, and Singapore. The likelihood that a Black American will murder a White American is 65 times greater than the likelihood that a citizen of Singapore will be murdered at all. Black men between the ages of 18-24 commit murder at a rate 175 greater than that of White and Hispanic women (and Hispanic women commit 85% of those murders). Between 1991 and 1994 they murdered at a rate of 350 per 100,000 populations, but were murdered at a rate of "only" 175 per 100,000. The other half of their murder victims were mostly White men. If such a high murder rate were to be sustained over the next 75 years (the average life expectancy in the US), then more than a quarter of all blacks in the US would have murdered someone (not including multiple murders by one person). Thanks to affirmative action putting the most incompetent bureaucrats in charge of our justice system (which reduced our "clearance rate" for murder to an all time low) more than a quarter of a million murderers have never been brought to justice just in the last 30 years, and most of them are black. Of the 25,869 homicides in the US in 1993 reported by the National Center for Health Statistics, only 16,297 were resolved, leaving 9,572 murderers Scot free, to murder again, and again.

When No Trouble Don't Produce Trouble

We have 3.7 unresolved homicides per 100,000 populations which is more unresolved murders per capita than the above countries have total murders per capita. Had the US homicide rate remained at its already high rate before the first of our 22,000 gun control laws was passed in 1965, there would have been 550,000 fewer homicides since then. The problem is not ownership of firearms by Whites--it is ownership of firearms by blacks who cannot be entrusted with that right--not in Africa, and not in the US. While Whites are a significant percentage of the victims of the ownership of firearms by blacks, blacks are an even bigger percentage. While Whites are a significant percentage of the convictions which were based solely on the existence of these 22,000 unconstitutional gun control laws (and not on an actual crime), blacks are an even bigger percentage of these convictions. Black Americans must recognize this, and understand that the ownership of firearms by blacks creates multiple problems: Created a requirement for 22,000 unconstitutional gun control laws. Undermined the spirit and intent of the Second Amendment. Assured that these gun control laws could not and would not work. Impaired the ability of all law-abiding citizens to defend themselves. Paralleled an almost tripling of the murder rate in the US. Enabled young American black men to achieve the world's highest sustained non-combat homicide rate. Contributed greatly to the murder of almost 0.2% of young black men each year. Put one million black men behind bars, more than are behind bars in all of Africa. Black people in general have sunk into a mire of behavior that leaves the average Joe/Jane scratching their heads profusely trying to figure out these strange new mannerisms from a perspective of logic and reason. You see, when you remove logic and reason out of the equation, the way that most black people behave today appears to be normal.

Don't Give The Beast The Advantage

It is only when you inject logic and reason back into the mix are you then forced to be honest and truthful and call out the behavior for what it really is. The focus of black people ideally should be to clean up that which is dirty within the community however instead most black people seem to think that the solution is to hide the dirt, refrain from addressing it and shoot down anybody who points out that there are some issues within the black nation that need to be dealt with. This is yet another example of the modern day black mindset of stupidity and foolishness and most black folks today are proud to be a part of an embrace this mindset with happiness and open arms. The first step towards restoration is actually admitting that there is a problem. Most black women and men have yet to even acknowledge this step forward. The black nation is trundling backwards rapidly and it is because of all of the above foolishness and more why we have not made any significant steps of progress within the last 70 years. Whether black folks like it or not, all of the above are signs of being effeminate. There is no reason for black boys and black men to be wearing pink in any garment, pink has always been and always will be a girl's color and no pink clothing promoting rappers are going to change this. This is the problem with this victim mentality, folks seem to think that they can do anything and that everything is ok. No everything is not ok and a man wearing pink as far as I am concerned indicates some serious underlying issues with that man. Why are you wearing skin tight jeans like a women black men? Since when was this deemed acceptable and who gave you that memo? This is simply yet again another classic sign of decadence among the black nation. Your trousers are supposed to be slack and of a loose fit. As ever, the so called Negro following and copying his European counterpart. I never thought in a million years that I would see this kind of clothing being sported by black folks in the US but it has happened for sure.

When No Trouble Don't Produce Trouble

Most black people by now have been informed as to where the sagging trousers phenomenon originated from yet many black folks especially the youth still embrace and exercise this act of stupidity, decadence and homo eroticism. Why black males who claim that they are not homosexual still hold the desire to show the whole world their underwear is beyond me. In cases like this you simply follow what black men do not what they say as following the words and not the actions will leave you as mentally confused as they are. I hope you black men and boys who sag your trousers realize that when you walk down the streets in that fashion, homosexuals are have a field day looking at you rear end and wishing that they could dive in and indulge. If that is the type of attention that you want to draw to yourself then that is your business however, do not expect me to take the same route. My trousers will remain firmly around my waist where they are supposed to be positioned and where they belong. Many young Black men feel angry and are desperate because Black communities and America have failed them. While some of this hopelessness is understandable because of their extreme negative circumstances, it does not give any young Black man the right to hurt others. Let's begin with a controversial question: Are young Black men doing the work of the Ku Klux Klan as the primary killers of Black people in America? Without much debate, the answer is yes! Although the impetus for Black-on-Black destruction differs from the Klan's motivation, the results are arguably more horrific. Judging strictly by the numbers, the Klan was never as efficient as young Black men are today at killing Black people. According to a study from the Tuskegee Institute, the Ku Klux Klan killed 3,446 Black people in America during an 86-year span compared with Black men who kill about this same number of Black people every six months.

Statistics from the United States Department of Justice clearly show the magnitude of this tragedy on U.S. soil, especially when compared with war- In two U.S. wars, 6,754 American soldiers were killed (including 2,019 soldiers in Afghanistan since 2001 and 4,735 soldiers in Iraq since 2003). Statistics show that more than 7,000 Black people are murdered in this country every year! During the 9-1/2 years the U.S. has been at war overseas, about 67,000 Black people were murdered in the United States. Most of these homicides were committed by Black men, primarily men in the 17-44 year-old age range, against other Black men in that same age group. Black men comprise about 6.5 percent of the U.S. population and nearly half of U.S. homicide victims. Today, the Black community faces a serious irony. Little more than 50 years ago, Black communities wanted Black men to protect them from White men who wore "hoods" while they killed Black people and destroyed their property. Fifty years later, Black communities are asking local (mostly White) police departments and state National Guard units to protect them from our sons and neighbors: mostly young Black men in "hoodies" and ski masks who are killing Black people and destroying their property. Whether perpetrated by the Ku Klux Klan or by young Black men, this terrorism is decimating Black communities. Opportunities for positive community development and growth are smothered when young Black men murder other young Black men and inadvertently maim and kill other innocent people in these communities. Children are afraid to travel to and from school, middle-income Blacks refuse to reside in high-crime communities, business owners steer clear of inner-city areas and senior citizens become easy prey. Black communities become paralyzed and implode under the weight of Black-on-Black crime, violence and murder. Five strategies, outlined by the U.S. Centers for Disease Control and Prevention, seem to offer the best approach to reduce youth violence and produce long-term, lasting, positive results.

When No Trouble Don't Produce Trouble

These recommended strategies include: (1) Build strong families and communities and employ responsible parents as the chief agents to reduce youth violence; (2) Teach young children ways to resolve conflict peacefully; (3) Provide mentors to serve as guides and role models for positive youth behavior; (4) Reduce social and economic causes of violence in young people's environments; and (5) Ensure spiritual or character-based training for young children and reinforce that training throughout their early teen years. Where is the official U.S. government's response to 67,000 Black American citizens slaughtered in its streets during the past 9-1/2 years? Implementing solutions that effectively address this reign of death in the Black community will not and should not come primarily from Washington, state capitals or city halls. While it is the Black community that must strongly respond with effective solutions and actions, government still has a crucial responsibility to support structural remedies to this genocide. So far, local, state and federal governments alike have answered with a "calculated non-response" to the national carnage and human catastrophe of this Black-on-Black murder. This same calculated non-response was the position taken by all levels of government during the reign of terror by the Ku Klux Klan. More than 145 years after the Klan's founding, only the killers have changed—not the killing, not the victims and not the poor response from government! Are young Black men doing the work of the Ku Klux Klan? They are doing it better than the Klan! And the world is watching. It is noted that although the reasoning for Black-on-Black killings may differ from the Klan's impetus, the results are in some black leaders words "arguably more horrific." The dates, parallel time lines, and related numbers sadly but factually speak for themselves. Noting a Tuskegee Institute study, a newsletter revealed that the Ku Klux Klan killed 3,446 Black people in America "during an 86-year span" as compared with Black men who kill about the same number of Black people "every six months."

Don't Give The Beast The Advantage

Backing up a Tuskegee documentation with this findings, authors Molefi K. Asante and Mark T. Mattson in their work "Historical and Cultural Atlas of African Americans" list that between the 29 years of 1889 and 1918 in the then 48 states from Alabama to Wyoming, 2,932 Black people were lynched. Comparatively, with our current 2010 Black-on-Black homicide stats, the authors chronicle the decade between 1890 and 1900 "as the most dangerous time" in the post Civil War era for Black men to be alive. They add that nearly 1,700 persons were lynched in that decade compared to 921 in the decade between 1900 and 1910; 840 from 1910 to 1920, and nearly 400 between 1920 and 1930. Again, comparatively speaking, that would be 3,861 Black people killed by white hands between the 40 years of 1890 and 1930; still on the low end when measured against current day reported Black killings by Black hands. Statistics from the United States Department of Justice demonstrates the shockingly overwhelmed magnitude of this Black-on-Black reality during the nine-and-a-half year period from 2001 through 2010. In two U.S. wars, 6,754 American soldiers were killed including 2,019 soldiers in Afghanistan since 2001 and 4,735 soldiers in Iraq since 2003. Shockingly for our nation's central city communities, the newsletter released data would reveal that during this same nine-and-a-half years that the U.S. has been at war oversees from 2001 through 2010, approximately 67,000 Black people were murdered during this same time in the United States. Yet another observer of stats comparing the killings of the Ku Klux Klan and the still growing Black-on-Black homicidal numbers is Clinton L. Black in his 2007 work "Why All Black People Are Coming to an End." According to his figures, the Ku Klux Klan lynched 3,437 Black men, women and children in the 115 years from 1866 to 1981. Today, he writes, Black people are murdering 3,437 Black men, women, and children in a 115 day period. Noting his findings, mathematically he postures that a Black person commits a crime against another Black person somewhere in America every second.

When No Trouble Don't Produce Trouble

His figures conclude that at this rate, that would be "six Black-on-black crimes a minute, 3,600 Black-on-Black crimes an hour, 86,400 Black-on-Black crimes a day, 604,800 Black-on-Black crimes a week, 2,629,743.83 Black-on-Black crimes a month, and 31,556,926 Black-on-Black crimes a year." The author contends that although the overwhelming majority of these crimes go unreported, this is still the most "devastating force" against Black people in the world today. Let's look at the numbers. For the purpose of this writing, we will use and anchor Black Star's figure of 67,000 Black-on-Black killings. Reviewing Black Star's Tuskegee figure of 3,447 Blacks killed by lynching, Black hands murdered 63,554 more Black folk then did whites during this present day period. Taking a look at Asante and Mattson's research of killings where 2,932 Blacks were lynched by whites. Black hands today murdered 64,068 more Black folk then did whites during the 29 years between 1889 and 1918. Since the U.S. has been at war oversees where approximately 6,754 American soldiers were killed, Black hands murdered 60,246 more Black folk then the numbers of reported Americans who died in Afghanistan and Iraq citing Black Star figures over the past nine-and-a-half- years from 2001 through 2010. And finally, we do not want to exclude author Clinton L. Black's findings. According to his figures, the Ku Klux Klan murdered 3, 437 Black men, women and children. Black hands killed 63,563 more Black people within the past 10 years than did the Klan over the 115 years from 1866 to 1981."The largest group responsible for homicides in this country is that of Black males in the 20 to 24-year age range. And their victims are similarly young Black men – a fact which has as its most tragic consequence that homicide is listed as the number one cause of death among Black males aged 15 to 30." We have top the Black-on-Black homicide rates of 67,000 Black people between 2001 through 2010 or the stat reflecting that as of 2007/08, Black males in the U.S. having the lowest graduation rates ever amongst Black males as well as the College level.

"Black students nationally score are at rock bottom on SAT and ACT with no outcry or action from leaders or parents." These scores "predict" low college admission rates, high unemployment rates and high incarceration rates. Black students are in trouble!" As well as the Black Community is in trouble and a positive and prideful Black future is in serious danger. What is more concern is why is it that for decade, we are continually witnessing the black community and particularly our children dying as a result of a slow but readily visible, understandable, and predictable self-imposed genocidal decay in our social, educational, political, and economic infrastructure while many of our so called black leaders, our ministers, our educators, our politicians, and our community stakeholders are saying and doing absolutely nothing. 145 years following 1865's Emancipation Proclamation, we can no longer use as an excuse or blame racism or White Supremacy for our Black community ills "WE CANNOT". While some disparities remain, things have generally advanced for Black people in America and today they are advancing still. Our President Barak Obama and Oprah are held up as proof. But have things really moved forward? Is this society actually becoming "post-racial"? The answer to that question can be found in every corner of U.S. society. Take employment: Black people remain at the bottom of the ladder, if they can find work at all. While many of the basic industries that once employed Black people have closed down, study shows employers to be more likely to hire *a white person with a criminal record* than a Black man without one, and 50% more likely to follow up on a resume with a "white-sounding" name than an identical resume with a "Black-sounding" name. The rate of unemployment for Black men is fully 48%. Or housing: Black people face the highest levels of racial residential segregation in the world—shunted into neglected neighborhoods lacking decent parks and grocery stores and often with no hospitals at all.

When No Trouble Don't Produce Trouble

Black people, as well as Latinos, who had achieved home-ownership had their roofs snatched from them. They were the ones hit hardest by the subprime mortgage crisis after having been targeted disproportionately by predatory lenders—resulting in the greatest loss of wealth to people of color in modern U.S. history. Or healthcare: Black infants face mortality rates comparable to those in the Third World country of Malaysia, and African-Americans generally are infected by HIV at rates that rival those in sub-Saharan Africa. Overall the disparities in healthcare are so great that one former U.S. Surgeon General recently wrote, "If we had eliminated disparities in health in the last century, there would have been 85,000 fewer black deaths overall in the early 2000's." Or education: Today the schools are more segregated than they have been since the 1960s with urban, predominantly Black and Latino schools receiving fewer resources and set up to fail. These schools more and more resemble prisons with metal detectors and kids getting stopped and frisked on their way to class by uniformed police who patrol their halls. Often these schools spend around half as much per pupil as those in the well-to-do suburbs. Or take imprisonment: The Black population in prison is 900,000, a tenfold increase since 1954! And the proportion of Black prisoners incarcerated relative to whites has more than doubled in that same period. A recent study pointed out that "a young Black male without a high school degree has a 59 percent chance of being imprisoned before his thirty-fifth birthday." On top of all that, and reinforcing it, is an endlessly spouting sewer of racism in the media, culture and politics of this society—racism that takes deadly aim at the dreams and spirit of every African-American child. And who can forget the wave of nooses that sprung up around the country, south *and* north, in the wake of the 2007 struggle in Jena, Louisiana against the prosecution of six Black youth who had fought back against a noose being hung to intimidate them from sitting under a "whites only" tree at school?

Don't Give The Beast The Advantage

All this lay beneath the criminal government response to Hurricane Katrina in 2005. For reasons directly related to the oppression of Black people throughout the history of this country, and continuing today, African-Americans were disproportionately the ones without the resources to get out of the way of that storm, as well as the ones concentrated in the neighborhoods whose levees had gone unrepaired for years. Far from "mere" incompetence, the government responded with a combination of gun-in-your-face repression and wanton, murderous neglect. People were stuck on rooftops in 100-degree heat for days on end, with nothing to eat or drink. Prisoners were left locked in cells as waters rose to their necks. The protection of private property and social control was placed above human life. The governor of the state ordered cops and soldiers to shoot on sight "looters"—that is, people trying to survive and to help others. On at least one occasion, people trying to escape the worst-hit areas were stopped by police at gunpoint from crossing over to a safer area. When evacuations finally *were* carried out, they were done with the heartlessness of a cruel plantation owner. Families were separated, with children ripped away from parents. Tens of thousands were scattered all over the country with one-way tickets, sometimes not even told their destinations. Back home, bodies were left floating in water, or lying on sidewalks, underneath debris, decomposing and mangled, for months. Through it all, politicians and commentators spewed out unrelenting racism. " A 10-term Congressman took the prize for declaring, "We finally cleaned up public housing in New Orleans. We couldn't do it, but God did." Incredibly enough, these slaves were denounced as "lazy" by the parasitical slave masters whose great wealth the slaves created through their back-breaking labor! These lies served both to "justify" the horrors of slavery and formed a crucial element in the "social glue" that held society together. This pattern, and this lie and its social use, have continued in different forms up to today.

When No Trouble Don't Produce Trouble

The fact that these supposedly "inherently inferior" people had played a crucial part in building up highly developed societies and cultures in both Africa and the Americas, long before Europeans came to dominate these places, was an "inconvenient truth" written out of the official histories and textbooks. And the fact that all human beings are all one species, with only relatively superficial differences in some characteristics, was also written out, with spurious racist pseudo-science substituted instead—lies that also come up in new forms today. There was nothing inherent in Europeans that led to capitalism taking root there first—there were a number of areas in the world where capitalism might have taken off slightly earlier or slightly later if things had come together a little differently. But Europe is where capitalism did take off, and the dominance of the capitalist nations of Europe and then the U.S. (and Japan, which developed in a different set of circumstances) over the past five centuries is inconceivable without slavery. Slavery fueled the foundation and rise of not just capitalism in general, but the U.S. in particular. This is not just a "stain" that can eventually be washed, or even scrubbed, away within the confines of this system; it is embedded in the very fabric of this society—indeed, the U.S. Constitution itself legally institutionalized slavery and deemed African-Americans to count as only 3/5 of a white person for census purposes. There is a semi-official narrative about the history and the "greatness" of America, which says that this greatness of America lies in the freedom and ingenuity of its people, and above all in a system that gives encouragement and reward to these qualities. Now, in opposition to this semi-official narrative about the greatness of America, the reality is that—to return to one fundamental aspect of all this—slavery has been an indispensable part of the foundation for the "freedom and prosperity" of the USA.

The combination of freedom and prosperity is, as we know, still today, and in some ways today more than ever, proclaimed as the unique quality and the special destiny and mission of the United States and its role in the world. And this stands in stark contradiction to the fact that without slavery, none of this—not even the bourgeois-democratic freedoms, let alone the prosperity—would have been possible, not only in the southern United States but in the North as well, in the country as a whole and in its development and emergence as a world economic and military power. Obviously, the way in which agriculture in the South developed was directly related to, indeed founded on, the system of slavery. But, beyond that, the way in which the U.S. related to the world market, and built up its prosperity and economic base in that way, was to a very large degree dependent on slave-based production. The interchange between the development of manufacture in the North and the development of agriculture in the South, for example—even when, before the Civil War, that interchange went to a large degree through the world market and through England in particular, where for example cotton would be sold to the textile mills in England and other products would be sold from England to the northern manufacturers in the U.S. —even that would not have happened in the way it did, on the kind of scale it did and with the prosperity that it led to, without slavery. Of course, this process—where, for example, cotton from the southern U.S. was to a large degree sold to England, rather than to New England—contributed over time to sharpening the contradiction between the slave system in the South and the developing capitalist system in the North of the U.S. But the point to emphasize here is that, in an overall and fundamental sense, the slave-grown products of the southern U.S. constituted a major factor in the development of the U.S. economy, in the North as well as the South. And the development of that economy, in turn, has been the essential underlying basis for the massive military machinery which is the ultimate enforcer of the role of the U.S. as a major world power.

When No Trouble Don't Produce Trouble

This poisonous master-class mentality did not die with the abolition of slavery—it continued, in new forms. In particular, each wave of immigrants that came over from Europe had to "fit itself into" the dominant relations of American society—they had to find an "economic niche" (usually toward the bottom rungs of the working class, at least at first) and they had to work out a relation to the dominant political and cultural superstructure of society.

In doing so, these white immigrants often tried to distinguish themselves from Black people—and this often exploded into the open antagonism of white mobs rampaging against Black people and even lynching them—yes, in the northern cities as well as the South, as these immigrant communities defined themselves as "full-blooded" white Americans *in violent opposition* to Black people. This system reinforced the master-class mentality among northern whites with petty, but not insignificant, privileges in jobs and housing. And this became a major double-barreled shotgun for the capitalist ruling class: it blinded these white people and immigrants to their most fundamental interests as members of the proletariat, turning their anger away from the system that actually exploited and oppressed them, and turning it against the most oppressed and exploited people in society. And it gave them an "identity" as *white* Americans, with a set of expectations and entitlements to go with it—and to defend. A minority of whites opposed this madness, and took up revolutionary or radical or even just decently humane positions; but while very important—and we'll return to its significance later—this sort of stand was far too uncommon. (A secondary, but important, effect of this master-class mentality among whites of all classes was to partly obscure the *class* character of the oppression of the masses of Black people—their position and role as viciously exploited *proletarians*, within the overall working class of the U.S.—and the many and close links between this *class exploitation* of large numbers of Black people, as part of the proletariat, and the *national oppression* of Black people as a people.)

Don't Give The Beast The Advantage

To return again to the period of slavery, it is important to be clear on an essential truth: the slaves fiercely resisted this. In the U.S. alone there were over 200 slave revolts, and the slaves of Haiti stunned the world when they successfully waged a 15-year revolution against first their colonial masters, then the British, and finally Napoleon's armies. Even with these heroic revolts, it was only with the Civil War that the resistance finally bore fruit in the U.S., and the emancipation of Black people from outright slavery was achieved. Here too the masses of Black people—both runaway slaves and "freedmen"—played a crucial role. When finally allowed to join the Union Army, they died at twice the rate of white soldiers (while being paid lower wages for most of the Civil War)! The Civil War itself came about because of the clash between two different economic and social systems: slavery, based on plantation farming in the South; and capitalism, based on factory and other wage-labor centered in the North. Most of this was in the form of small concessions—not only did this not begin to touch the real scars of hundreds of years of terrible oppression, but discrimination *continued* in all of these arenas. Nonetheless, these advances were hardly insignificant. Even more important than these particular concessions, in some ways, were the "intangibles." The consciousness of not just African-Americans but other minorities, and many millions of white people as well, radically changed. People sharply challenged the lies that for decades had been taught in American schools and had been driven home in American culture through works like *Gone With the Wind* and *Birth of a Nation*. The REAL history of slavery, the Civil War, Reconstruction, and the whole period of the 20th century began to be unearthed and brought forward. The '60s showed that a movement that had Black people as its most solid base of support and the struggle for their emancipation as its leading edge, and that drew connections to other outrages of the system and other struggles against that system, could also inspire and draw forward people of other oppressed nationalities within the U.S., students of all nationalities, and then spread as well to women, to white proletarians ("poor whites"), soldiers and beyond. All kinds of people began to look at everything about this society with fresh eyes—and with the blinders suddenly taken off, they didn't like what they saw and decided to question it and fight it! To put it another way, the '60s showed that when masses rose up in rebellion against the powers-that-be, and when that was coupled with a political stance that called out the system as the problem, and when a growing section of that movement linked itself to and learned from the revolutionary movement worldwide...well, when all that happened, you could radically change the political polarization in society. What could hardly be imagined yesterday suddenly became a real possibility for tomorrow, which demanded action today. (Some of these same phenomena, in microcosm, also occurred in the Los Angeles Rebellion of 1992, over the acquittal of the police who had beaten Rodney King. While the initial spark came from the Black masses, significant numbers of Latinos and whites, especially the youth, either joined in or politically supported it, and many, many people were at least temporarily drawn into political life and some to a much more radical and even revolutionary political outlook.) Today, *as they did in slavery times,* the capitalist ruling class builds up the church as the MAIN institution in the Black community. Government money that once went to public education and community arts is now channeled through preachers who align themselves with the government and with the Christian fascist movement that has been built up by Bush. Nowhere is this sharper than in the prisons. The struggle of the '60s spurred among prisoners a thirst for knowledge and truth, and they fought for and won the right to take college courses and have access to literature even though they were locked up;

today that is increasingly suppressed and flushed away while reactionary fundamentalist "prison ministries" are given total access to the minds of the literally millions of Black youth whom the system shuttles through these hellholes, with large numbers at any given time serving long sentences in degrading prison conditions. While many religious people and clergy oppose, and can be united in struggle against, the outrages and crimes of this system, and important aspects of the oppression of Black people and others, there must be struggle and debate over the real character of the problem and solution, and the worldview and method that is necessary to win complete emancipation, and the real role of religion in relation to all that. Religion—both in general and particularly in the more recent period—plays the role of turning people away from seeking a real understanding of the actual causes and dynamics of things, as they really are, and the possibility of changing things in this real world. Even when more "progressive" versions of religion may encourage people to resist oppression (or particular aspects of oppression), it still promotes the idea that, when all is said and done, people themselves cannot change things by consciously seeking out and coming to an understanding of what is the problem—what is the actual cause of people's situation and where oppression actually comes from—and waging a determined struggle on the basis of that understanding, but instead they must ultimately put things "in the hands of a god" and rely on this non-existent god(religion as a god) to give them the courage and strength to persevere. And things are worse, on a whole other level, with the reactionary religious viewpoints that openly uphold this system and the key pillars of its oppressive relations. The challenge has to be made: get out of trying to make it in "the game" which this demonic system has given you to play and in which you'll never be more than a pawn, used against the very people you come from; get into something that can finally bring an end to the long dark night brought down on people by that system.

When No Trouble Don't Produce Trouble

Rupture with the kill or be killed mentality and the mindset that comes with "the game"—and unleash what "the game" has suppressed: the aspirations for freedom and Holy emancipation for *all* people that have been buried but not killed...and the deep desire to turn your anger and daring where, and against whom, it should and must be turned to realize *those* aspirations. Get out of seeking to get over on and even killing people just like you—and get into fighting the demonic powers today, as part of getting ready for this Holy revolution, and as part of transforming the people to make that Kingdom Community. There were glimpses of this potential in Hurricane Katrina, when people in "the life" sometimes risked all to save someone from a different "set," and in some of what happened in the 1992 L.A. Rebellion, when gang antagonisms were temporarily put to the side. There was more than a glimpse in the '60s, when people broke out of the criminal life and into the revolutionary movement. And there must be much more of that in the community today—brought forward by the righteous in Christ, and all who come to deeply understand that a radically different future is possible, with this becoming in turn a tremendous force of inspiration for millions more...*not* in some scheme to "stop the violence" that cannot work in this demonic system, and *not* in a gang truce that can never be more than a truce but in a righteous Kingdom Community aiming to change everything. Yes, there are difficult challenges in building and maintaining GOD's Kingdom Community here on earth today. But to think that one can emancipate humanity without confronting challenges this tough and far tougher is to turn away from reality. And that we cannot do, and do not need to do. We have the tools to biblically understand the world and society, to figure out why things happen and how to change them, and to bring out of that a new world; we have to join together and use them. To be very clear: none of this will come easy. It will entail tremendous struggle and sacrifice, and it will only come about amidst great upheaval and even death and destruction—

Don't Give The Beast The Advantage

brought about largely by the forces seeking to keep in effect the old order of oppression and exploitation—which will of necessity be part of finally overthrowing and doing away with this demonic system upon Christ return. It will entail tremendous struggle and sacrifice, and it will only come about amidst great upheaval and even death and destruction—brought about largely by the forces seeking to keep in effect the old order of oppression and exploitation—which will of necessity be part of finally overthrowing and doing away with this demonic system upon Christ return. But this struggle and sacrifice can, at long last, serve to completely sweep away the chains of oppression that have bound so many for so long, and bring about a true Holy emancipation. Such a righteous community would be greeted with joy in every corner of the world and inspire hundreds of millions, throughout the globe, to take up this cause that the "Kingdom Message" reach the four corners of the earth. Amen!!

CHAPTER IV

Good Cop, Bad Cop

Few play the blame game or point-the-finger exercise quite so avidly as the black community. Few have evolved such an advanced culture of victimhood from which their overdeveloped sense of grievance and entitlement has grown. They have the same education and opportunity as anyone else, but—oh no—they are special, are downtrodden, are misunderstood. It must be atone of respect the black community because we exist. But because of gangsta rap and many other social issues. Because young men wear hoods or carry knives or manage to walk in a menacing pimp roll. It is thought respect had to be earned. Should a young black be excluded from school, it is not because he is lazy, disruptive, or stupid, but because the education system is against him. Should the police stop him, it is not because he acts suspiciously or his kind commits most robberies, but because the police are inherently racist. Should he fail to gain a job, it is absolutely the employer's fault and not because the applicant was sullen, lippy, and barely house-trained. So it goes on. And on and on, complaint rather than effort and attainment has become the cultural norm.

Don't Give The Beast The Advantage

The liberal apologists are ever there to explain away and facilitate the mindset. Just like Muslims who will not accept Jihadist extremists draw on the Islamic faith or environmentalists who cannot admit population growth is a key root of global warming, so few in the black community—even when the evidence is plain, even when the police run Operation Trident directly to tackle black gun crime—will put up their hands and say with honesty: "We have a problem and it is our own fault and our responsibility." To utter such words would be construed as heresy, would be to stray from the adopted consensus that every ill, every crime, every mishap within the black community is due to slavery and oppression by the whites. No matter slavery in Britain was abolished in 1833—we must still suffer the rage and allow plasma-screen televisions and top-of-the-range footwear to be looted from a burning store. It is fine to smash a shop front when insurance or the taxpayer will help the owners restock. It is fine to ruin a livelihood when you have no concept of earning. It is fine to take something that is not yours when it is on display and your logic tells you, you can have it. It is said that this is what the sixty-year experiment in state handouts has achieved. The work is available if the indigenous black population seeks it. Indeed, Britain brings in tens of thousands of Gambians and Ghanaians and other migrants to staff hospitals and care homes and fill a "labor shortage" that does not exist. In accepting that Afro-Caribbean's have not needed to work, colonialism have entrenched them in their postcode gangs and their ghetto. Slowly they say police and social services are gone. Education used to be the way up and the way out. Not much more. A generation of blacks feels no need, does not see the point, has no fathers or family to kick their backsides and tell them to strive. After all, it is so much easier to smoke weed, to shoplift, to snatch a purse or bag, to hold a knife to a throat and rape a "some gal."

If all they are told is that they are the victims, the Earth's rightful inheritors, and that cash can be generated without much effort, then they will follow their peers and the path of least resistance. The young offender institutions are full of them. Certainly there are lawyers speaking to the account, How much trouble is too much for a police officer? How should departments deal with the "bad boys/girls" in their agencies? Different officers experience disciplinary problems on the job for different reasons. Sometimes the problem is the officer; sometimes it's the department; often it's a little of both. Therefore, a range of intervention options must be available to address not just officer attitude and behavior, but organizational practices as well. The basic message is: Law enforcement discipline rarely has to be all-or-nothing and most problem officers can be salvaged if treated correctly.

DE-SELECTION

Of course, the best way to prevent police misconduct is not to hire problem-prone officers in the first place. If only it were that simple. Much of the selection process for police candidates is actually de-selection, or *screening out*, of potentially troublesome candidates based on a variety of practical and psychological criteria. An alternative approach to selecting candidates is the screening in of those individuals who are suitable and desirable. The problem is that most current screening protocols typically focus on identifying the characteristics of "bad" officers; much less is currently known about what traits make a "good" officer and about how career experiences affect these characteristics. Moreover, even the best pre-employment screening protocol cannot necessarily anticipate emotional and psychological problems that may develop after the selection process, during an officer's tenure on the force.

Don't Give The Beast The Advantage

Nevertheless, certain index signs are useful. Screening-out red flags include drug or alcohol abuse; behavioral disorders due to serious medical or psychiatric disability; a history of serious juvenile delinquency; repeated conflicts with authority; misconduct or poor performance in former jobs; chronic financial problems; or a criminal record. A particularly important feature of the evaluation is the candidate's style of handling anger and aggression, both in the past and presently. Indeed, these are basic criteria for almost all types of employee screening, but especially for those positions that concern public safety. Formal personality testing per se typically screens out about 15 percent of police candidates. Screening-in protocols should assess not just behavioral styles and character traits, but the potential for both formal training and learning from experience. Especially for modern professional police forces, there is growing recognition of the value of problem-oriented policing and the need for patrol officers to possess good overall intelligence, especially abstract reasoning, mental flexibility, interpersonal creativity, and problem-solving skills. Other related positive traits and qualities include psychological maturity, common sense, reliability, conscientiousness, and the ability to apply discretion in an ethical and equitable manner. The challenge is to find or develop selection measures and protocols that can accurately identify and predict these positive traits. Yet even the best screening protocol is really only a behavioral snapshot of the officer's psychological qualifications at the beginning of his or her career. Ideally, evaluations and reassessments should be a regular component of an officer's progress through his or her law enforcement career. Such reassessments should be balanced with monitoring, training, and supervision safeguards throughout the officer's tenure with the department.

EDUCATED COP

Certain skills and traits are largely innate: you either have them or you don't. Many skills, however, can be taught to varying degrees, depending on the individual. The general training model employed by most police academies is based on principles of adult learning that involve a combination of didactic classroom instruction, behavioral participation, simulated patrol scenarios, and role playing. The emphasis is on developing a range of both physical and psychosocial intervention skills that assume frequent, and often unpleasant, interactions between citizens and police. Such exercises are most effective when they focus on learning to anticipate problems before they arise and generating productive and flexible problem-solving strategies as an alternative to the use of force.

MANAGING CONFLICT

 enhances officers' communication skills as the primary tools for controlling potentially violent citizens. To be sure, nonviolent tactics won't always work, and officers must be competently trained in how and when to use appropriate physical force when necessary. The guiding philosophy comes from the martial arts concept of true strength emanating from inner confidence, peace, and wisdom; of power as a tool that is best used quietly; and of true respect inhering as much in force restrained as in force expressed. Such a model might be practically reinforced by training in communication skills that appeal to this kind of "verbal judo" approach. For police trainers, this translates into helping officers learn to depersonalize the unavoidable insults and verbal attacks by citizens that come with the job of community policing. Even if every officer cannot be expected to become an adept street-corner psychologist, diplomat,

POLICE COUNSELING

or philosopher, most officers can at least be trained to view alternatives to force as a means of safe, effective policing. Coaching and counseling represent a more focused, individualized application of education and training that directly addresses a particular officer's problematic behavior in the context of supervision. Coaching and counseling both require constructive confrontation of the officer's behavior, but it is important to realize that confrontation need not – indeed, *should not* – ever be unnecessarily hostile, offensive, or demeaning. Professionalism and respect can characterize the interaction of a superior with a subordinate in any supervisory setting, including coaching, counseling, discipline, or even termination. The focus is on correcting the problem behavior, not bashing the officer. Supervisors should be firm but civil, preserving the dignity of all involved. The difference between coaching and counseling lies in their focus and emphasis. *Coaching* deals directly with identifying and correcting specific problematic behaviors. It is concerned with the operational reasons those behaviors occur and with developing specific task-relevant strategies for improving performance in those areas. Most of the direction and guidance in coaching comes from the supervisor, and the main task of the supervisee is to understand and carry out the prescribed corrective actions. For example, an officer who fails to complete reports on time is given specific deadlines for such paperwork as well as guidance on how to word reports so that they don't become too overwhelming.

Good Cop, Bad Cop

An officer who behaves discourteously with citizens on patrol is provided with specific scenarios to role-play in order to develop a range of responses for maintaining authority without abusing the public.

1. Identify and define the problem.

2. State the effect of the problem.

3. Describe the desired action.

4. Make it attractive.

5. Document and summarize.

There are a limited number of issues (matters of trans-jurisdictional concern) in policing, and there are only about ten (10) or so main areas of scholarly interest in the field known as police science. Police organization & management; styles of policing; operational strategies; police use of technology; socialization into the police culture, including recruitment, selection, and training; use of force; police dangers and stress; police ethics; accountability of police to the public; and multiculturalism in policing.

POLICE MANAGEMENT

History has shown, time and time again, the disastrous consequences of bad police management. Police managers include any sworn rank above that of sergeant and/or any sworn or non-sworn administrators. This isn't just an issue of who gets promoted or the unique stressors at each rank - although those are important areas of research in themselves. It's more a problem with the shape of the organizational pyramid -- always a hierarchy with the chief at the top and rigid chains of command flowing to the bottom.

Several experts have suggested the pyramid needs to be inverted, with the community at top, followed by line officers, then managers. Police organizations are *tall, closed, hierarchical, paramilitary bureaucracies*, and for the most part, organizational theory holds that this combination represents the worst of management science. Police managers serve as a citizen's gateway to the criminal justice system. This is reflected in the experience of being told "that's not a police problem", which a management decision is, with line officers simply relaying what their supervisors will or will not accept. In actual fact, it's probably the line officer and the citizenry who should be deciding what a police problem is. Unfortunately, the bureaucracy gets in the way by: (1) limiting ingenuity -- no lower level employee gets to use their particular skills, ideas, or talents; (2) limiting contact with the community -- a pseudo-professional distance develops between people and the police; and (3) limiting contact within the department -- employees in one area don't know what employees in the other area are up to.

Delegation of authority is supposed to make the system work. The chief delegates authority to commanders, who delegate authority to managers, and so on down the line. Written guidelines in the form of policies and procedures also regulate conduct. However, delegation only seems to work in small-to-medium departments where everyone is alike and a generalist. Large police departments have precincts, divisions, bureaus, and specialists where authority cannot be easily delegated. The fact is that real authority only passes down thru those who fit the mold of a uniformed street cop. Another problem (or perhaps not a problem at all) is the growth of generalists who compete with specialists in police organizations. A police style is how each department and officer view their particular mission or purpose and identify with particular methods or techniques to fulfill that purpose.

At the departmental level, style reflects the historical legacy of the agency, and to a lesser degree, the sociodemographic characteristics of the population it serves. At the individual officer level, style reflects "grace under pressure", or what has developed in the person as the best part of their philosophy of policing or the "war stories" that make up the symbols of what they see as good police work. Other definitions of style exist, but these are as good as any. The first person to study style was Wilson (1968), and his typology of three styles remains useful today. Each department usually has one of three styles, although some may be a mix of two. The three styles are: (1) watchman; (2) legalistic; and (3) service. Briefly, a watchman style is generally found in poorer communities and emphasizes informal police intervention - persuasion, threats, roughing up - rather than arrest because the priority is maintaining order. A legalistic style is a commitment to enforcing the letter of the law and frequent use of arrests in a focus on community safety, but takes a hands-off approach to community problems that are not crimes. A service style is bent on helping the community by working hand in hand with social service agencies, and by using referrals rather than arrest. Other models of police work have been suggested by Kleinig (1996) who proposes that police departments tend to think of themselves in one of the following ways: (1) *crime fighters* - using the military model to portray criminals as the enemy or bad guys and police as the good guys; (2) *emergency operators* - using the firefighter model to portray themselves as emergency handling professionals who just happen to be competent at crime control; (3) *social enforcers* - using the band-aid model to portray themselves as fixer-uppers who settle things once and for all by force if necessary; or (4) social peacekeepers - using the peacekeeping model to portray themselves as pacifiers of the populace, bringing peace and psychologically satisfying closure to social conflicts.

Individual officer styles have been proposed by Broderick (1977) and Muir (1977). Broderick's typology is based on respect for due process, and consists of: (1) enforcers - with little respect for due process; (2) idealists - who want to keep the peace but respect due process; (3) optimists - who emphasize due process; and (4) realists - who don't seem to care about anything, much less due process. Muir's typology is based on passion to use force, with what he calls professionals and enforcers who use force, and reciprocators and avoiders who avoid force. Some criminal justice experts find the study of police style to be a futile attempt to stereotype or pigeonhole departments and officers. Others find it an illuminating and useful area of study. A strategy (as opposed to a tactic) is a long-range goal or plan designed to bring about some particular accomplishment or outcome. Strategies are always practical or operational in character, but often have long-term impacts on both the agency and community. Most strategies can be identified with the time periods when they were popular. A strategy popular in the 1960s, for example, was police-community relations. Abbreviated and known as PCR programs, this was a strategic approach to getting people to respect the police again (since the 1960s were characterized by riots and hatred of police). Specific operational forms of PCR included ride-along (so people could spend a day seeing what police went through), and open houses (so people could come inside police stations and see there were no dungeons, torture chambers, or the like). Some PCR programs still exist, such as neighborhood watch, Officer Friendly (DARE) programs, Police Athletic Leagues (midnight basketball), and property engraving services.

During the 1970s, police experimented briefly with team policing, an idea thought to have originated in Aberdeen, Scotland, but took different forms in America. In some places, it was a demilitarization movement, getting rid of uniforms and replacing them with stylish civilian blazers. In other places, it was the elimination of detectives (who make up 15% of an average department), and giving patrol officers the authority to do detective work. In most places, however, it involved officers being semi-permanently assigned to particular neighborhoods, to get to know the local people and problems intimately. In the 1980s, police tried different variations of patrol strategy. Directed patrol was tried, where police concentrated their patrol time in areas that crime analysis showed were hot spots. Aggressive patrol was tried, which is the same as roadblocks or crackdowns. A few places tried foot patrol. Other places tried split-force policing, known today as differential response, which is when half the patrol cars are committed to certain problem areas and the other half can respond to calls. The 1980s also saw widespread abandonment of two-person patrol cars. The 1990s have been characterized by two strategies: problem-oriented policing, the idea that police find out what is causing citizen calls for service, or the crime problem; and community policing, a philosophy of cooperation with citizens on what citizens regard as their problems and needs. Research on the effectiveness of police strategies has produced mixed results, although it looks like the general trend toward more community involvement is here to stay. The 21st Century saw the birth of homeland security policing, which had some situational awareness features like community policing, but also had strong federalization or centralization features.

Don't Give The Beast The Advantage

Policing has always been technology-driven. For example, inventions such as radio, telephone, and automobiles have profoundly shaped police work. Computers and forensic techniques, however, have a long way to go (although there are some sparkling examples of high-tech computing and forensic labs in some places). Even today, one might find police departments that still use typewriters, Vascar (a low-tech version of radar), and have no idea how to collect and process DNA. Fairly rapid progress is being made, but the main problem, as most experts see it, is that police are interested primarily in technological advances that deal with weapons, armor, SWAT-like stuff, and newer, better ways of taking people down to control and detain them -- as opposed, unfortunately, to technology that might get at the root causes of crime and allow police to work smarter, not harder. For example, a police officer might never complain about the battery life on a laser-guided handgun, but one minor glitch in a software program that analyzes crime hot spots and the whole idea of using computers to do better police work is thrown out the window. There is a certain ambivalence about technology in police work, and the legal system, culture, and academia to some degree reinforce the notion that police ought to be nothing more than "super-sentinels" who used nothing more than their God-given, yet highly-trained human senses to catch criminals. Anything else might be unfair, and no one wants the police turned into some domestic monitoring organization, although this is all changing in the homeland security era. No other occupation has had their culture and personality more thoroughly analyzed than the police. In all fairness and frankness, attention in this area is rather embarrassing, but reveals some unpleasant facts. First of all, there's the problem of recruitment. Recruits generally come from the blue-collar labor force or the military, people who are tired of being carpenters, plumbers, truck drivers, or contractors, and soldiers who have been steered into police work by military tradition.

The cause may be because newspaper ads for police jobs are typically placed in the unskilled or skilled labor sections of newspapers, but it represents a serious problem because it means police have never figured out how to recruit from college campuses, the private security industry, or places where women and minorities might be found. Following recruitment is selection. Some good people are weeded out from police work because of unfortunate accidents with the law, drugs, or their credit history. Some police departments can't hire the foreign-language speaking officers they need because of naturalization requirements. Some people, with disabilities, could easily do the work, but at best, only get conditional offers of employment and/or a finding that reasonable accommodations cannot be made. Vision requirements prohibit some from even applying. The physical fitness standards are very tough. After selection comes training, a formal course of study at police academy, which is often nothing more than fourteen weeks of boot camp. After the academy, there's still a probationary period of field training, where they're told to "forget all that stuff learned at the academy." On the job, there are few opportunities for in-service training, other than watching videos or the occasional workshop. The process of socialization, defined as learning the values, symbols, and beliefs of a group takes place throughout recruitment, selection, and training. Add attitudes to what is learned, and you've got what is called a subculture. The police subculture has been characterized long ago by Skolnick (1966) as consisting of the qualities of danger, authority, and isolation. Everything that is important to believe in (to become a police officer) revolves around sensing danger, how to exert authority, and keeping quiet about police business. Experts have been warning for years that this kind of police subculture has got to change because it's a ready-made recipe for excessive force against citizens.

Socialization results in personality change, or at least a working personality that one puts on for short periods of time. Few souls have enough hardiness to avoid falling into habits of behaving, knowing, and moralizing that accompany development of the police personality. Using a trait approach to the study of personalities, experts have consistently found anywhere from 6-13 dominant traits among police. The following table is a list of those traits: *Dominant Personality Traits of Police Officers Authoritarian, Suspicious, Insecure, Honorable Cynical, Hostile, Loyal, Secret Conservative, Individualistic, Efficient, Prejudiced and Dogmatic.* Nothing defines the central role of police in society better than its monopoly over the unquestionable use of force. Aggressiveness, toughness, relentlessness, and (one might say) a cult of violence all tend to permeate the adrenaline-soaked nature of police work. A couple of horrific examples where the monopoly on force was abused would include the Abner Louima case in 1997, where the aggressive tactics of New York City's Street Crimes Unit (SCU) involved rectal damage on a suspect with a toilet plunger. Over a two year period, the SCU unit processed 45,000 people with their get-tough methods. Another example would be the Amadou Diallo case in 1999, where an immigrant who fit the profile of a serial rapist was shot 41 times after reaching for his wallet. Extreme examples such as this are called illegal use of force, where criminal and civil liability issues arise. About two million people a year are subjected to police force if we include aggressive handcuffing along with rough physical touching and verbal threats. Weaponless tactics are the most common use of force, and it occurs most frequently when alcohol, drugs, or mental illness are involved on behalf of the suspect. A small percentage of officers appear to be over-represented among the more extreme incidents of force. It makes sense to refer to excessive force as what some individual officers do and excessive use of force as what is practiced on a department-wide basis.

There is no inherent connection between the two, as at the department-level, there may be good policies regulating use of force thru specific "rules of engagement" (which are what separate police action from military action), but at the individual-level, there may be instances of discretion abuse and/or situational variations.

In an average year, 600 suspects are shot and killed by police, while another 1,200 are shot and wounded, and 1,800 are shot at and missed. Black property offenders are twice as likely as any other group to be shot at by police, and another interesting statistic is the growing percentage of cases (over 10%) that involve suicide by cop, where a note is usually found saying "Sorry to get you involved. I just needed to die."

Criminal justice experts are divided over whether racial differences exist with respect to police use of force. On the one hand, the Christopher Commission (1991) stated that white officers were somewhat more likely to use excessive force against African-Americans, and watchdog groups like the ACLU, Amnesty International, and Human Rights Watch have stated a pattern exists, but on the other hand, respected researchers like Adams (1996) and Tony (1995) as well as the U.S. government itself have never unveiled a pattern. There are some unique dangers and stressors that police officers must face. Some people are not cut out for the work, and others are. The job sometimes takes away the best of them. Many officers meet their death while performing police work. On-the-job deaths occur from stress, training accidents, auto crashes, and at the hands of criminals. Law Enforcement Officers Killed in the Line of Duty have averaged 150 a year until the year 2001, when it jumped to over 200 (the most frequent causes being terrorist attack, criminal gunfire, and auto accidents). Studies by the FBI have not found that slain officer's differ in any respect from non-slain officers. They were well-liked, friendly, and easy-going.

Officers are often exposed to blood and other bodily fluids that transmit serious diseases like AIDS. While only a couple cases of officers contracting the disease are known, precautions are necessary at crime scenes, when frisking suspects, collecting evidence, and such things as the emergency delivery of babies in squad cars. It's exposure to risks and dangers like these that may contribute to alcoholism or drug abuse. Other officers report family stress, or the problems of trying to hold together a police family, hence, divorce rates are unusually high among police officers, although this may qualify as a myth more than fact. Others suffer heart disease or gastrointestinal disease. The most debilitating stress in police work may come from the fatigue of working long hours around the clock, such as at a disaster or rescue scene where there is repeated exposure to carnage and suffering. Shift work in policing is also stressful. Fatigue contributes to accidents, injuries, and misconduct. Another source of stress is the criminal justice system itself. Police are accustomed to getting things done, and seeing something happen for the good of society. Unfortunately, not all arrests lead to conviction, not all evidence is admitted in court, and not all punishments are harsh enough. Police experience a terrible sense of helplessness and powerlessness when they see repeat offenders back on the street and victims go without justice for the harm done them. It's this kind of stress that is associated with police suicide, which is twice the rate of the general population. The oldest problem in law enforcement is corruption, but other misbehaviors are of concern, ranging from use of profanity to sexual deviance.
Is it feasible to expect untarnished "goody two shoe" behavior, all the time, from every police officer? Codes of ethics are either aspiration hopes and dreams or regulatory codes of conduct, and most professions in the U.S. use the aspiration variety. This allows us to use words like fidelity and integrity as unreachable goals with no practical ideas on how to achieve them.

However, the movement for training in police ethics is growing, and it is based on the idea that police officers need to hold themselves to higher standards than is expected of the average person. Yet, it is unclear if police will hold themselves to higher or lower standards than the average person. Much evidence suggests that lower standards may be entrenched. For example, a large majority of police would probably agree with the following statement by General George S. Patton:

"When I want my men to remember something important, to really make it stick, I give it to them double dirty. It may not sound nice to some bunch of little old ladies at an afternoon tea party, but it helps my soldiers to remember. You can't run an army without profanity; and it has to be eloquent profanity. An army without profanity couldn't fight its way out of a piss-soaked paper bag. As for the types of comments I make, sometimes I just, by God, get carried away with my own eloquence."

The problem of ethics is not so much an individual matter as an issue of professionalization. A group with professionalization (as opposed to just being a profession) possesses a special morality that attaches to its social roles rather than the people who inhabit those roles. Mere professions can be created by certification, licensure, or continuing education, and anybody can create a code of ethics. Some of the defining qualities of professionalization include: a monopoly over an essential public service (and police certainly have that, but must work to maintain that trust); a regulatory code of ethics (one that guarantees the public the exact standards by which services are delivered); special knowledge and expertise (never a resort to plain old-fashioned common sense); higher education (not just training, but lifelong learning); autonomy and discretion (the ability to make judgments and be creative rather than rule-driven); and self-regulation (successfully earning the right to say that outsiders can never appreciate the constraints and pressures of police work).

75
Don't Give The Beast The Advantage

The basic reason why policing has remained unethical and sub-professionalized is because police have demanded self-regulation instead of earning it (they have also abused their monopoly trust and never made a dent in any of the other defining qualities of professionalism). Police power and authority exists not because of some inherent quality of the office, but because power and authority exist as social relationships or a characteristic of society. People comply with authority because they believe that those who exercise authority know what they are doing with it. People in positions of authority are therefore accountable to those who (continuously, socially) give them authority. Therefore, it is an incumbent duty of the police to arrange accountability mechanisms for the public, to assure the public that the police know what they are doing. Accountability is not the same as liability. Suing the police for damages isn't going to change anything or lead to reforms that makes the police more willing to open themselves up to self-examination, public inspection, or continuous improvement. The most common notion of accountability in policing - *what goes around comes around* - is seriously misguided. While some police may feel this belief in karma or superstition is an adequate reflection of justice in the real world, it (superstition) does nothing more than reinforce cover ups, festering grievances, and bad traits in the police personality. There are a variety of accountability mechanisms that the police could do. The simplest thing is to prepare annual reports (like corporations), and release them to the public and the media. These shouldn't be reports about crime rates going up or down, but reports about how citizen complaints were handled and the like. The next thing would be admission of errors in judgment. Nobody expects the police to be perfect, or never make mistakes. People are tired of the blue wall of silence and cover-ups. The police also should have rulebooks that are sensitive to different local and social conditions.

Good Cop, Bad Cop

One policy manual size doesn't fit all. Police should have civilian advisory boards that assist them with planning and the logical extension of this -- civilian review boards (replacing Internal Affairs units for the investigation of misconduct). The issues of diversity and multiculturalism make up the last topic here, and can be approached in different ways. Statistically, blacks make up 12% of all sworn officers nationwide and other minorities make up 8%. Women make up 13% of law enforcement. These are token levels, and it's also safe to say minorities and women are underutilized and under-promoted. Some experts have said that policing, following the military, is the world's most racist and sexist organization, but it's debatable over whether that's deliberate or not, intent being a key element of racism and sexism, unless recourse is made to improbable concepts like latent or institutional racism. For example, let's take the notion of racial profiling; a late 1990s phenomenon defined as any police action that relies on race, ethnicity, or national origin rather than behavior or information in identifying a criminal suspect. Racial profiling goes in many areas of government and business, and in the most common variety of its practice, it leads police to stop and inspect selected people passing through public places — passengers on airplanes, drivers on highways, pedestrians in urban areas, visitors crossing national borders — because they fit a statistical profile based on group membership. Racial profiling is quite different from psychological profiling, but the technique can be traced to drug courier profiling, a DEA technique developed in the early 1980s to spot traffickers at airports. Arguments in favor of racial profiling include the statistics that blacks are 13 times more likely to be carrying drugs than whites, which minorities have higher offender rates, and communities are much safer when police focus their efforts on high-incidence and high-prevalence areas and people.

77
Don't Give The Beast The Advantage

Arguments against racial profiling include the statistics that most people do not favor, statistical-driven police work leads to stereotype-driven police work, it is morally and ethically wrong, and it generates a public perception of policing as biased. Of these, perhaps the strongest argument is public perception of bias, because most of what passes for multicultural policing is not substantive, but appearance aimed at improving public perception of the police. In the end, it may be that "PERCEPTION" is all that matters.

BEING BOUND

Somewhere in just about every person is the longing to give kindness, to be diligent, to do great work and to make a difference in life. Sadly, those longings are often deeply buried by fears, insecurities, doubts, mistrust . . . . disillusionment and so much more. Life doesn't always unfold the way you want. It can in fact be very messy, inconvenient and uncomfortable.

What people say, what people do, and what they say they do are entirely different things. The purpose for life is to live it, to taste the experience to the utmost, to reach out far beyond what you see, without fear for a newer and richer experience. "Life is a process of becoming, a combination of states we have to go through. Where people fail is that they wish to elect a state and remain in it. This is a kind of death." The meaning of life is creative love. Not love as an inner feeling, as a private sentimental emotion, but love as a dynamic power moving out into the world and doing something to make an impact.

Every man has an obscure respect for life in others, especially if it is moral life, the rarest and most difficult sort of bravery in a Man is not to be bound the thoughts that makes him become the very brute the world understands that this man is an immoral man.

A Man is not bound to win, but A Man is bound to be true. A Man is not bound to succeed, but A Man is bound to live by the light that he have. A Man must stand with anybody that stands right, A Man must stand with Man while he is right, and Man must part with that Man when he goes wrong.

Perhaps love for your fellow Man is the process of leading A Man gently back to the image in which A Man is bound to..."THE IMAGE OF GOD".

Rev. Anthony Martin-

A MESSAGE TO THE COMMUNITY

To the People of the Community…Good Cop….Bad Cop and Government…you must exercise restraint against the innocent foolish ways, you must exercise compassion for the poor in spirit, you must exercise control of your own temper, you must exercise meeting one to the level of one's thinking, you must exercise a clear conscience from home life toward the Job. You must exercise public office as to denying yourself and not into your temporal ways and means as you are in the home life. You must exercise Life over Death in your community; you must exercise productivity over producer of trouble, you must exercise Love is patient, you must exercise kindness. You must not exercise envy, you must not exercise boasting, you must not exercise being too proud. You must not exercise dishonor toward others, you must not exercise self-seeking, you must not exercise easy angered emotions, and you must not keep any record of wrongs. You must not exercise delight in evil but rejoices with the truth. You must exercise in every way protection of the community, you must exercise trust, you must exercise at all times hope, and you must exercise at all times perseverance. You must exercise the love that never fails. "When I was a child, I talked like a child; I thought like a child, I reasoned like a child. When I became a man, I put the ways of childhood behind me. For now we see only a reflection as in a mirror; then we shall see face to face. Now I know in part; then I shall know fully, even as I am fully known. And now these three remain: faith, hope and love. But the greatest of these is "LOVE". 1 Cor. 13: 11-13.

Rev. Anthony Martin-

www.ingramcontent.com/pod-product-compliance
Lightning Source LLC
Chambersburg PA
CBHW052113070526
44584CB00017B/2469